SARTRE

回 回 回

This is a volume in a new series of PORTRAITS, devoted to figures who have changed the world we live in. The series is edited by Walter Kaufmann, Professor of Philosophy at Princeton University.

The first three volumes are:
> SARTRE *by Hazel E. Barnes*
> WITTGENSTEIN *by William Warren Bartley III*
> LENIN *by Rolf H. W. Theen*

They will soon be followed by:
> LUTHER *by Richard Marius*
> ENGELS *by Alfred Meyer*
> LINCOLN *by Hans Morgenthau*

Hazel E. Barnes

SARTRE

回 回 回 回 回

J. B. LIPPINCOTT COMPANY

Philadelphia and New York

U.S. Library of Congress Cataloging in Publication Data

Barnes, Hazel Estella.
    Sartre.

    Bibliography: p.
    1. Sartre, Jean Paul, 1905–
PQ2637.A82Z554   848'.9'1409   72–13764
ISBN–0–397–00750–7

Excerpts from the following books and periodicals are re-printed with the kind permission of the publishers:

Being and Nothingness by Jean-Paul Sartre, translated by Hazel E. Barnes, Philosophical Library, 1956.

"Itinerary of a Thought," interview with Sartre in *New Left Review*, 1969.

"Sartre Accuses the Intellectuals of Bad Faith," interview with Sartre by John Gerassi in *The New York Times Magazine*, October 17, 1971, © 1971 by The New York Times Company.

Search for a Method by Jean-Paul Sartre, translated by Hazel E. Barnes, Alfred A. Knopf, 1963.

CONTENTS

EDITOR'S·PREFACE

回 回 回

No philosopher in all of history has reached as large an audience in his lifetime as has Jean-Paul Sartre. Of course, he is not only a philosopher but also a playwright, novelist, and journalist, a writer of short stories, essays, and criticism, and an astonishing person. He is, in short, a philosopher in the French tradition—more like Rousseau and Voltaire than like most professional philosophers today. Yet his philosophical works are extremely difficult to read. Moreover, the relation of his fiction to his philosophy poses many problems, and there is no agreement as to whether his *Critique de la raison dialectique* ("Critique of Dialectical Reason," not yet available in a complete English translation) is consistent with his earlier existentialism. Has he given up existentialism to become a Marxist?

Hazel E. Barnes, a Professor of Classics, has translated into English Sartre's early *Being and Nothingness*, which established his reputation as an existentialist philosopher, and his later *Search for a Method*, an essay contained in the *Critique*, in which he disparages existentialism as "a parasitical system" while hailing Marxism as "the philosophy of our time." She has also written a large book on *Humanistic Existentialism* in which she relates the fiction of Sartre, Camus, and de Beauvoir to their philosophical writings. Her other works include *An Existentialist Ethics*.

The present book does not concentrate on Sartre's life and personality because he himself has written a celebrated autobiography covering his early years, and Simone de Beauvoir's three-volume autobiography also deals with Sartre. Only the first chapter of this book is devoted to the man and his life. The bulk of the book deals with the development of his thought and tries to demonstrate its essential unity. Only a scholar who is thoroughly at home in the whole corpus of Sartre's voluminous writings could have accomplished such a difficult feat.

WALTER KAUFMANN

1

INTRODUCTION

回 回 回

Outline of a Life

Jean-Paul-Charles-Aymard Sartre was born in Paris on June 21, 1905. His mother, Anne-Marie, was the daughter of an Alsatian, Charles Schweitzer, and first cousin to Albert Schweitzer. Jean-Paul's father was a young naval officer, Jean-Baptiste Sartre, the son of a country doctor. At the time of his marriage to Anne-Marie, he was already ill with a fever he had picked up while on duty in Cochin China; he died the year after Jean-Paul was born. Mother and child took refuge at the home of her father at Meudon in northern France.

Years later, in his autobiography, *Les Mots* (*The Words*), Sartre wrote that the death of his father "was the great event of my life." [1] This was not because the dead man as remembered exerted any influence on the child; quite the contrary, he was all but forgotten in the Schweitzer household, apparently even by his widow. In his son he failed to awaken so much as curiosity. Not callously but with disconcerting frankness, Sartre ascribes to his lack of a living father certain qualities in himself which obviously he looks on with favor. Because he was not forced to learn filial obedience, he never developed the desire to wield authority or the thirst for power. His life, without the burden of parental

[1] *Les Mots* (Paris: Gallimard, 1964), p. 11. Translations of Sartre's writings, unless otherwise indicated, are my own.

pressure, has possessed a certain "lightness." Sartre writes, "I willingly subscribe to the verdict of an eminent psychoanalyst. I have no Superego." The death of Jean-Baptiste "returned my mother to her chains and gave me freedom" (p. 11).[2]

Charles Schweitzer treated Anne-Marie and Jean-Paul as if they were two children together. The boy could not see his mother as an authority figure, nor was there any need to run to her for protective affection. His childhood was dominated by his grandfather, an indulgent tyrant who assigned to his grandson the role of pampered prodigy. Jean-Paul was only too glad to comply. Even his early and genuine love of books was intertwined with the desire to impress and win praise. At the age of seven he was reading *Madame Bovary*, which fascinated him though he could not really understand it. But at the same time he publicly read Flaubert and other literary giants in the Schweitzer library, he was secretly reading "real things"—adventure stories—behind his grandfather's back. Before long he took to writing them. For the child, literature was already an absorbing occupation, a way of escape from loneliness, and a destiny. By means of it he saw himself as one who had been endowed with a mission; he envisioned his future life as a preparation for going to join the great immortals.

In 1911 the family moved to Paris, where Charles Schweitzer opened the Modern Language Institute. Sartre has commented wryly that not only were the majority of the students Germans who wanted to learn French by the direct method but many of his father's associates and friends were from Germany. Yet Sartre had been taught to hate the Germans, "who robbed us of Alsace." This discrepancy between the abstract enemy

[2] This and the following page numbers refer to *Les Mots*.

and living human beings had already been impressed on him during occasional visits of the family with their "German" relatives at Gunsbach in captive Alsace.

A more consequential contradiction in family attitudes stemmed from religion. Charles Schweitzer was Protestant. His convictions were not so strong as to prevent him from allowing his Roman Catholic wife and daughter to bring up Jean-Paul in their own faith. At the same time, he indulged his anti-Papist prejudices by continually ridiculing everything connected with Catholicism. The grandfather's rationalism won out. Without trauma, with no emotional conflict or strain, Sartre, aged twelve,

decided to think about the Almighty. Suddenly he tumbled into the blue and disappeared without offering any explanation. "He doesn't exist," I said to myself with polite surprise, and I believed the matter settled. In a way it was, since I have never had the slightest temptation to resurrect him. [p. 209]

Sartre claims that in his devotion to literature he retained the religious dimension. Though he had got rid of God, the Holy Ghost remained in the form of a sacred mandate to the Writer. It was not until he was almost fifty that Sartre, abandoning his faith in literature as a self-justification for the writer, felt able to say that he had seen his atheism through to the end.

The adult Sartre deplores his childhood even as he recognizes that it led him by a straight path to the career which has brought him fame and, in recent years, a position from which he can act on the stage of world politics. It was certainly a strange sort of boyhood Sartre spent there in that house, "alone with an old man and two women." Thoroughly spoiled and quite content to accept his grandfather's judgment of him as a true picture, Jean-Paul was apparently insulated against some of the shocks which would have proved traumatic to many children. When Charles Schweitzer finally entered his eight-year-old grandson in the Lycée Montaigne, he persuaded the authorities to enroll the boy in one of the higher classes. The first day's exercises resulted in the humiliating decision that he must be demoted. Schweitzer, enraged at the stupidity of the school's personnel, removed the boy for private tutoring. Jean-Paul was serenely undisturbed; he was a child prodigy who couldn't spell, that was all. Nor was he dismayed when later at a public school in Arcachon his grandfather's influence won him special treatment. Jean-Paul sat at a special desk next to the teacher's rostrum and remained there even during recess periods. He found it all quite legitimate and "distinguished to be bored at the side of M. Barrault" while his boisterous classmates played games outside (p. 63).

There was another side to all of this. At home he lived with boredom, loneliness, and an unidentified sense of being an empty sham. On their walks in the Luxembourg Gardens, neither mother nor child could disguise the fact that Jean-Paul was totally rejected by his peers. And it hurt. Too proud to beg, he would gladly have given up all his privileges in exchange for an invitation to play even the role of a dead soldier in the children's games. "I had met my true judges, my contemporaries, my peers, and their indifference condemned me. I was shocked at the discovery of myself through them: neither a marvel nor a medusa, just a little shrimp of interest to nobody." [p. 110]

Early adolescence was especially unhappy for Sartre. His mother had remarried in 1916; the following year

Sartre went to live with the couple in La Rochelle while he attended the lycée there. He did not get along well with his stepfather and felt a certain inner estrangement from his mother. Contat and Rybalka record that at this period he systematically stole from his parents—money and even books which he sold secondhand.[3] At school he was a mediocre pupil who did not mingle with his schoolfellows.

In 1920 (Sartre was now fifteen) things began to grow better. He left La Rochelle to return to the Lycée Henri IV in Paris, where he began to distinguish himself as a student. Short pieces of his were published in various literary reviews. Most of these juvenilia have been lost. The most significant was a short story, "L'Ange du morbide," which is still available to us.[4] It is a somewhat self-conscious, satirical narrative of an aesthete school-teacher who cultivates his inclination for the morbid and decadent. He plans the seduction of a young girl in the late stages of tuberculosis but retreats in horror when, as he tries to kiss her, she is overcome by a coughing fit and spits blood. Terror-struck by the thought that he may have contracted the disease, he seeks reassurance from specialists, then marries a cowlike country girl of impeccable good health and chooses a new career of bourgeois respectability as far removed from decadent sensibility as possible. The story anticipates Sartre's novel *Nausea* in some ways and also the story "Childhood of a Leader." It satirizes both literary affectation and bourgeois com-

[3] Michel Contat and Michel Rybalka, *Les Écrits de Sartre. Chronologie, bibliographie commentée* (Paris: Gallimard, 1970), p. 22. This book lists year by year the events of Sartre's life and supplies relevant bibliographical information concerning his writings, lectures, and interviews.

[4] Contained in Contat and Rybalka, *Les Écrits de Sartre.*

placency, and it describes the kind of self-deception which Sartre afterward made famous as "bad faith."

In 1924 Sartre competed successfully for admission to the highly selective École Normale Supérieure de la rue d'Ulm, where he studied in preparation for the *agrégation de philosophie*, the degree required for persons wishing to teach in French lycées and universities. There is evidence that at least by the next year Sartre, who was now about twenty, already had in mind the germ of his later philosophy. In two unpublished letters to a friend, he developed the idea of "the contingency of consciousness as an emptiness in being." [5] It is impossible that this position could have represented even the skeletal outline of the theory fully developed later in *L'Être et le néant* (*Being and Nothingness*). Too much of that work is inextricably mingled with the ideas of philosophers with whom Sartre was virtually unacquainted in 1925. Nevertheless, it is evident that Sartre gradually built his own philosophical system around his original insight, adapting, modifying, and—from his point of view—correcting the positions of existentialist and phenomenological philosophers as he encountered them in the years subsequent to his student days in Paris.

Sartre has remarked that his French education was strongly dominated by Cartesian rationalism. Indeed, the inheritance from Descartes is obvious in the very fact that he makes inquiry into the nature of consciousness central to his whole position. He criticizes Descartes for not going far enough, for having set forth as the irreducible *cogito* (the "I think") a consciousness which was already complex—both reflective and personal. Sartre's attempt to go back behind even "I think, therefore I am" as starting point may rightly seem to introduce a radical

[5] *Ibid.*, p. 23.

separation from Descartes. Still the Cartesian *cogito* as lucid, reasoning consciousness is omnipresent in *Being and Nothingness* and is perhaps the primary influence in keeping Sartre the most rational of all existentialists.

Sartre failed his first attempt at the *agrégation* in 1928. A year later he took first place. Simone de Beauvoir, who had studied for the examination along with him, was second. It is primarily because of her that we have so vivid and detailed an account of the personal side of Sartre's life from the time of their first encounter in 1929 until the early 1960s (the last volume of her autobiography was published in 1963).[6] The long association between the two, though highly idiosyncratic, stands as a monument to the possibility of significantly satisfying human relationships. Long before either of the pair had made any meaningful political commitment, they were rebelling against the conventional traditions of bourgeois institutions, among them the sanctity of marriage and family. At the outset Sartre proposed to de Beauvoir a private "two-year contract." Later on it was she who indignantly rejected his suggestion that perhaps they might marry after all. Since then, although maintaining separate residences and allowing to one another complete freedom to develop other erotic attachments, they have lived and worked together more closely and obviously with more sympathetic understanding and pleasure in each other than one is likely to encounter in most supposedly ideal marriages.

After an unwelcome term of military service (he refused the opportunity of officers' training) Sartre accepted a teaching position at Havre, a provincial town

---

[6] The three autobiographical volumes are *Mémoires d'une jeune fille rangée* (1958), *La Force de l'âge* (1960), and *La Force des choses* (1963). All have been published in Paris by Gallimard.

on the northern coast of France, to which he later paid
dubious tribute by using it, under the pseudonym of
Bouville (Mudville), as the setting of *Nausea*.

In 1933 Sartre was awarded a fellowship at the In-
stitut Français in Berlin. His decision to go to Germany
for this year of study is undoubtedly the most important
single event in the history of his intellectual development. It was there that he became thoroughly acquainted
with German philosophy (even Hegel was neglected in
the French universities), and, most important, he discovered phenomenology and the work of Martin Heidegger. Sartre's debt to phenomenology can be measured by
the fact that the subtitle of *Being and Nothingness* is
"A Phenomenological Essay on Ontology." Sartre em-
braced *in toto* the phenomenological approach: to study
direct conscious experience, independent of any commitment one might make as to the nature of existence as
such, and to treat objects in the world solely as they reveal themselves in their appearances to consciousness.
Sartre found in the work of Edmund Husserl the method
he required to support his own view of consciousness; yet
it was his break with Husserl which launched Sartre as
an independent and original philosopher. He discussed
the point of disagreement in his first significant philosophical essay, "The Transcendence of the Ego." [7]
Sartre rejected Husserl's notion of a "transcendental
ego" or structured, personal consciousness as responsible
for the ordering of conscious activity. Sartre wished to
keep consciousness free of anything that would predetermine the nature of its experience; for him consciousness is not an entity but a free process. To support his
argument, he developed the idea that consciousness in-

[7] "La transcendence de l'Égo." Written in 1934, this essay
was first published in *Recherches Philosophiques*, VI, 1936–37.

volves the introducing of a psychic distance or Nothingness between itself and its objects. We have seen that he
had been working toward this position for some years.
For its full philosophical formulation, Sartre borrowed,
built on, and considerably modified Heidegger's concept
of Nothingness as a basic ingredient of human
experience.

The influence of Heidegger's *Being and Time*
(1927) is unmistakable in *Being and Nothingness*
(1943).[8] *Dasein* (the human existent) as a creature of
inner distances, the individual life seen as a perpetual
projection of oneself toward the future, the idea that my
Past comes to meet me out of the Future, the view that
my body is an instrument in a hierarchy of instruments
—these are but a few of the themes which link the two
books together. In a lecture in 1945 Sartre defended his
own existentialism as "a humanism" and explained that
the one premise common to all existentialists is the belief that "existence precedes essence." The individual is
radically free. He exists first, then makes himself by his
choice of action. For the religious existentialist, only the
immediate subjective encounter with God and the personally experienced truth are valid measures of authentic existence. For the humanistic branch, man (and
every individual man and woman) must take on his
shoulders the total responsibility for his life and for the
history of the world; there is no supernatural or transcending impersonal truth to serve as criterion. In this
discussion Sartre placed himself with Heidegger as an
atheistic existentialist in contrast with religious thinkers
such as Kierkegaard and Marcel. He appears to have
irritated Heidegger more than he pleased him by such

[8] The years listed here are original publication dates, not
the dates of English translations.

acknowledgments. Two years later in the famous "Letter on Humanism" Heidegger explicitly dissociated himself from Sartre and from existentialism. He was certainly correct in indicating that the gulf between his philosophy and Sartre's was too great to be ignored. Even at the time of the publication of *Being and Nothingness* one might argue that the similarities between the two were less pronounced than the differences. All the same, Heidegger's subsequent disavowal must have resulted, at least in part, from changes which had occurred in his own thought, drawing him away from existentialism toward what could more properly be called a philosophy of Being.[9]

After his stay in Germany, Sartre returned to Havre for two years, then went to teach in Laon for a year. In 1937 he was appointed to a position in the Lycée Pasteur in Paris. When war broke out in 1939, he was mobilized at once. After the fall of France in 1940, without ever having been actually under fire he was taken prisoner.

At this date Sartre had already published several important philosophical works, all of which foreshadow the philosophy of *Being and Nothingness*. Besides *Nausea* and his earlier youthful attempts at fiction, he had published several short stories which in 1939 were brought out in a volume entitled *Le Mur* (*The Wall*). In addition to their high literary merit, these are of interest in indicating the transitional nature of Sartre's thought in the nineteen-thirties. "Childhood of a Leader" serves almost as a fictional commentary on many passages in

[9] Sartre's lecture was published under the title *L'Existentialisme est un humanisme* (Paris: Nagel, 1946). Heidegger's "Letter on Humanism" appeared in *Platons Lehre von der Wahrheit. Mit einen Brief über den "Humanismus"* (Bern: A. Francke, 1947).

Being and Nothingness. Others reflect Sartre's study of earlier psychologists. "Herostratus" might almost be read as the work of a follower of Alfred Adler. "Intimacy" offers a classical pattern of Sartrean bad faith but reflects as well the ideas of Wilhelm Stekel on feminine frigidity. Absolutely none of the stories show any sign of significant political thinking on Sartre's part. We are told by Contat and Rybalka that in the mid-thirties he was "vaguely tempted to join the Communist Party," but he engaged in no political activity, preferring to express his anarchistic rebellion by refraining from voting in what he considered meaningless elections.

De Beauvoir has recorded her first recognition of a change in him. In February 1940 when Sartre came to Paris on a short furlough, she found him "firmly resolved not to hold himself aloof from politics any longer." His new ethical position was based on the notion of "authenticity." Sartre felt that he had an obligation toward the younger generation, who must not be let down like the "lost generation" after World War I. Every man, he declared, must make himself responsible for whatever situation he finds himself in and engage himself in some course of action. Specifically he outlined for de Beauvoir his views on the necessity for the writer to engage himself, a theme which Sartre developed in article after article in the early postwar period.[10]

From this point on, although de Beauvoir's autobiographies and the biographical information collected and minutely catalogued by Contat and Rybalka provide us with a wealth of detail concerning the external events of Sartre's life, we shall find his true intellectual biography in the works he has written. In seeking the man in his writing, we shall be following Sartre's own directions:

[10] *La Force de l'âge*, p. 442.

to come to know the author through his work rather than to try to explain his books by what we can learn of the man who wrote them. "It is *Madame Bovary* which illuminates Flaubert," he says, "not the reverse." [11]

Time and Paradox

In all discussion of Sartre, time is of the essence—Sartre's time and our own, the time of the world, and time as the life-form of human consciousness. It is man who brings time into being; his being *is* time. In describing the conscious individual, Sartre says of him that he is the one who, in the present, is not what he is (past) and is what he is not (future). We perpetually remake the meaning of the past in the light of the future which we are in process of choosing. Therein lies our freedom. History, defined in the present by the simple fact that something happens to people, is simultaneously "an orientation toward the future and a totalizing conservation of the past." Just as we are both agents and recipients of historical action, so we make time and are made by time. As an objective structure in the world, time by itself "steals" a man's action from him, betrays his intentions, alienates him from himself. In Sartre's philosophy, the "temporal ekstases" of consciousness and the world in which a person "inscribes his being" are inextricable. By understanding the way in which they are bound together, we can hope to grasp the intimate connections linking the anguished subjectivism of Sartre's fictional heroes, the individual analyzed in *Being and*

[11] *Critique de la raison dialectique* (*précédé de Question de méthode*) (Paris: Gallimard, 1960), p. 284.

Nothingness, and the Neo-Marxist analysis of society and history in Sartre's "Critique of Dialectical Reason." The treatment of time is one of the significant aspects of Sartre's fiction, whether his fictional work is viewed purely as literature or as offering illuminations (never, I think, mere exemplifications) of his philosophy.

For Sartre, time provides both continuity and rupture. Instants are not points of time or hard little entities which add up to those longer periods by which we measure a lifetime or the duration of a world. The present is lived as process, as a projection toward an always receding future. The instant stands there in my experience as a psychological threat—or promise—that at any moment it would be possible for me to insert an abrupt cleavage between the past as it seemed to me when I chose it and the past as I now view it in the light of an entirely different future from the one I projected earlier.

Then what of Sartre's own time? Do his life and work reflect any such revolutionary instants? How does he view his life?

In reading Sartre's autobiography, we are very much aware that his childhood has not simply been recorded; it has been weighed, analyzed, judged and fixed in time by the adult of near sixty, the Sartre who declared in 1964 that for fifty years he had "dreamed his life." The book is far less interesting as a source for factual details of Sartre's early years than as a revelation of the attitudes of the mature adult. Indeed, some critics have complained that the boy who actually lived the decade following 1905 never appears in the autobiography. Of course. But then would that child be of any interest to us except as the precursor of *our* Sartre? Our concern with him is the same as Sartre's. We look at him retrospectively as the first stages of becoming—that is, dialectically—and this is his only possible value for us.

Sartre has said that there are two basic attitudes which one may choose with respect to the events of one's life. We may ask to feel a solidarity with our past as if one simply spins out a continuous thread, like the caterpillar weaving a cocoon. Or we may feel that our life is a continuous flight from the past. Sartre has chosen the latter. There are at least two moments in his life which in his own eyes constitute a "radical conversion." He remarks, ironically, that he likes to think of his life as a continuous progress. Adverse criticism of his past behavior fails to touch or even secretly pleases him, for he feels detached from the man back there; on the other hand, he would be deeply hurt if someone could convince him that his earlier work was better than its sequel. More seriously, he tends to emphasize rather than to play down possible inconsistencies in his writings. At times his attitude toward an earlier work is almost one of astonishment. "It's incredible, I actually believed that!" he exclaims in 1969 apropos of comments he had made in the period immediately following the publication of *Being and Nothingness*. And he refers to that book, disdainfully but rather admiringly, as a "monument of rationality." He calls his biographical essay on Baudelaire "a very bad book." He has publicly reproached himself for remaining too aloof from the problems of his unhappy hero in *Nausea*, a novel in which, according to its author, he "gaily demonstrated the impossibility of living, without perceiving that [he] was caught up in that same impossibility." Sartre's 1964 explanation of the meaning of the line "Hell is others" in *No Exit* is so far from what the play appeared to be saying in 1944 that it is almost too good an example of his claim that we can freely remake the meaning of our past. Yet along with all this, Sartre adds that he has "changed, like everyone else, within a permanence." Indeed, Simone de Beauvoir, writing in 1963, says emphatically that Sartre has never abandoned the fundamental positions outlined in *Being and Nothingness*.[12]

It is not only Sartre who has changed. *The Flies* does not speak to us in the same accents now as it did in the early forties even though the text remains the same. Obviously, the implicit references to the Nazi Occupation have lost their urgency and have become part of the background information a teacher provides for young students. Still, the declaration that, once men and women know they are free, no oppressive government, no established system is unthreatened is perhaps more meaningful to today's revolutionary consciousness than it was—to unoccupied countries, at least—in the forties. The decisive difference lies in the thrust of the play's philosophical and religious impact. Students reading *The Flies* now are more irritated than shocked or delighted by Sartre's sly thrusts at the doctrine of original sin, divine miracles, and traditional arguments for the existence of God. The weight of traditional religion lies very lightly on the shoulders of most readers. In the forties, when Orestes strode forth in the wake of the death of God, he seemed to some a Nietzschean savior and to others an anti-Christ; in either case his revolt was a supreme humanistic assertion. Today the claims of religion are popularly viewed not as bonds with the past and with oppressive institutions but as the acknowledgment of an essential and life-giving mystery asserted

[12] The quotations and related points which are brought up for brief mention in this chapter will be discussed with appropriate documentation later.

against the scientific spirit of the last few decades. In the minds of the radical young, Sartre's atheism suspiciously resembles the rationalism which is believed to deny the validity of feeling and nonrational areas of experience. The positive significance of the play lies in its emphasis on the necessity for commitment, which, to be sure, has always been present; meaningful discussion centers around the question of whether Orestes' revolt and affirmation represent irresponsible individualism or the discovery that no one's personal freedom is either meaningful or justifiable until it is intermeshed with the struggles of all men and women.

How then should we situate ourselves in time as we seek to understand and evaluate Sartre's work? If we are at all persuaded by what he has written, we shall abandon any hope of finding a vantage point from which to grasp it under the aspect of eternity. Nor do I think it would be profitable, even if possible, to retrace Sartre's literary steps, considering each book in isolation, cut off from those future works which followed and from its own future. Yet some roughly chronological approach is necessary; otherwise we should be forced to choose between discussing only the most recent writing or restricting ourselves to an abstraction of those ideas which have remained steadfast without development. It is my intention, with regard to the early writings, to approach them somewhat as Sartre has dealt with his own childhood; that is, we shall try, so far as possible, to view them as they actually were—factually—but at the same time to see them in the light of what they became for Sartre, and for us too, at a later period.

Is there such a thing as a Sartrean system, a total *Weltanschauung?* Or do we confront, rather, the intellectual biography of a man who held a series of divergent, often conflicting, views? There have been abrupt shifts; that is undeniable. It is even possible, without falsifying, to contrast the Sartre of various periods in such a way that his most recent stance appears to be diametrically opposed to the Sartre of the late thirties. For example, it is a matter of record that politically Sartre has progressed from an attitude of nonengagement through Neo-Marxism to radical political activism. He has moved from an aesthetic purpose which came close to viewing literature as a way of salvation for the writer to the apparent abandonment of literature. To put it another way, he at first saw in creative writing a means by which he might escape from the meaningless contingency of this world. A few years later he was advocating "engaged literature" in which the author accepted the responsibility of changing the world so as to save others. In the early sixties he declared that the writer is not privileged and that there is "no salvation." Finally, in 1971 he is quoted as declaring that "the only viable activity for the intellectual today is the political tract." *Being and Nothingness* is concerned with individual subjectivity; man is radically free, a creator of values; he is morally responsible *for* his actions but *to* himself alone. In 1967 we find Sartre joining with Bertrand Russell in planning for the International War Crimes Tribunal which met at Stockholm to pass judgment on those who "have transgressed the laws of humanity." All of this cries out for some kind of explanation. Should we look for a radical conversion which, as decisively as Paul's experience on the road to Damascus, would cut Sartre's life in two? Or a steady, unified progression? Or is it rather that elements were there at the start which retrospectively make the development of Sartre's thought appear reasonable and natural if not predictable?

I am convinced that those who insist on a total break and inconsistency in Sartre's philosophy do so because they understand neither his fundamental ontology and psychology nor his later theory of society and history. Convinced that Sartre's view of consciousness allowed for only untrammeled subjectivism, "fictitious values" (whatever *they* are), and a wholly negative view of human relations, these persons are persuaded beforehand that any positive sociology and philosophy of history must by definition be inconsistent with Sartre's existentialism. It is significant that such critics usually do not approve of either "Sartre." They attempt to see him as first the proponent of a purely arbitrary, capricious, and irresponsible freedom and then as the advocate of a totalitarianism in which all freedom is lost. Yet it is just as mistaken to identify Sartre's political theory with traditional, established Marxism as it is to label his existentialism willful caprice. If there is misinterpretation at each end, no wonder the transition from one to the other appears difficult.

A comparable situation exists with regard to the relation between Sartre's philosophy and his literature. Obviously the aesthetic makes its own demands, and to insist that Sartre's imaginative works are to be read only as the embodiment of a philosophical message would be to condemn the fiction wholesale. But we do not need to follow the preposterous example of the English critic who claimed that philosophy "has perhaps always been something of a sideline for Sartre." [18] Nor should we fall into the opposite trap of concluding that

[18] Here, and in what has preceded, I am thinking especially, though not exclusively, of Mary Warnock's book *The Philosophy of Sartre* (London: Hutchinson University Library, 1965).

artistic needs have led Sartre to arrive at conclusions at variance with his true belief as expressed in the formal philosophy. The literature and the philosophy reinforce each other; only by studying both can we hope to grasp Sartre's total view of man's relations with the world. I believe strongly that what Sartre has given us is a unified and total view, even though the system as it stands today allows us to trace the stages of its growth, to discern false starts and unexpected turns of direction.

Since the keystone of Sartre's philosophy has been precisely his insistence on man's radical freedom and his ability to make a new "choice of being," we should hardly reproach him for having surprised us in his career as a writer. On the other hand, if we find that there is indeed a continuity, someone might argue that this fact in itself shows Sartre the philosopher undermining his theory by his life, which would seem to be a quite vivid demonstration that he is either wrong or in bad faith. As I interpret him, the developments in the later Sartre can be traced back to ideas latent or implicit in earlier formulations. At times he builds on them, either by extension or with new structures allowed but not really anticipated. On other occasions he has recognized difficulties in his own thought and hardened them, so to speak, by modification and movement in a different direction. An example of the first procedure is found in his concept of the "we." This was admitted only as an evanescent inessential structure in *Being and Nothingness* but takes on great significance in the concept of the group-in-fusion in the *Critique*. An example of the second is the "choice of being." While never rejecting it, Sartre realized that there were certain problems inherent in this notion even as he first proposed it. In recent psychological discussion he seldom speaks of it and takes as his central focus the "lived experience" (*le vécu*). This is to put at the center of psychic life an experience which is much more opaque and self-restricting than the choice of being; yet both notions represent man as internalizing and structuring the significance and meaning of the situation in which he finds himself.

I do not intend that we should conclude that in thus interpreting Sartre, we have simply found one more instance of the old adage, "The more we change, the more we become ourselves." My point is that Sartre's development has been neither inconsistent nor inevitable, certainly not predictable by him or anyone else, not even by hindsight. Sartre claims that an individual chooses from out of the many possible motives in a given situation those which will determine his future action. Every act is caused, but it is the agent who has chosen to establish one thing as a cause rather than another. Retrospectively we can imagine, for example, that the search for transcendent being which Roquentin pursues so nostalgically in *Nausea* could have been developed by Sartre into a doctrine of art for art's sake. After all, the search for a human essence brought Malraux ultimately to the "voices of silence" in marble and canvas, a recourse for which we might easily imagine his early fictional heroes would bitterly reproach him.

In raising the question of consistency in Sartre's thought, we shall, I believe, do him an injustice if we repeat the common procedure of simply setting summary quotations from one work side by side with those from another and attempting to judge their compatibility. Sartre is not exempt from the requirements of logical rationality any more than any other philosopher is. Yet just as we realize that Heraclitus deliberately employs contradictory statements in order to point to an existing harmony composed precisely of opposites, so we must realize that Sartre has, from the beginning, attempted to delineate the ambivalent, hybrid, contradictory quality of human reality. To rob consciousness of its ambivalence is to transform it from process to entity and thus falsify Sartre's position. In the *Critique* Sartre argues that it is dialectical, not analytical, reason which alone is capable of interpreting society and history, including the life project of the individual. While he makes no such claim in *Being and Nothingness*, here, too, we must be careful to grasp Sartre's thought in motion, as it were, rather than as a set of principles, each one of which may be considered separately in logical analysis.

Sartre's approach is characterized primarily by his constant use of paradox. At times he tries to capture the contradictions inherent in the human condition by juxtaposing them in a startling formulation; for example, his statement that the human being is not what he is and is what he is not. Or that the individual is always free but always "in situation." Or that consciousness causes there to be a world, yet "adds Nothing to Being." In such instances there is something to be explained—but not explained away—and Sartre elucidates with remarkable precision and clarity. More important and more difficult to grasp are the paradoxical conclusions which stand at the end of his description of man rather than as starting points. We are told that each of us spends his life trying to realize a missing God. The discussion of human relations pictures a multitude of solitary individuals, each one of whom is trying to realize the impossible goal of oneness with others. Over and over, the motif of human life is presented as a thrust toward a goal which is on principle unrealizable, toward a synthesis of contradictions which cannot be reconciled. An ideal completion is proposed which furnishes the *raison d'être* of the struggle and which would annihilate the strugglers if it could be attained. If we read these paradoxes as Sartre intended, then we shall find that despite all the emphasis on forlornness, nausea, and despair, Sartre envisions human life as creative process, a free bestowing of meaning where there would otherwise be chaos. If we realize that the paradoxes represent the first steps in a dialectic, we shall expect to see them caught up and developed in a broader view of the world in which the individual is a part of a whole without being lost in it.

The point at which I think we may profitably begin our examination of this development is the winter of 1940. At this date Sartre had already published a novel, a book of short stories, a few minor but significant philosophical essays. He had not yet completed *Being and Nothingness*. He himself was a prisoner of war in a camp in Germany.

2

THE DISCOVERY OF FREEDOM

With the approach of Christmas in the stalag, the prisoners received permission from the Germans to put on an entertainment. For the occasion Sartre wrote and acted in a play called *Bariona or the Son of Thunder*.[1] Until recently he refused to allow this play to be published, explaining that it was so intimately addressed to the special circumstances of its performance that it could not be properly understood apart from them. A note from Sartre accompanies the printed text. "If I took my subject from Christian mythology, this does not mean that the direction of my thought changed under captivity, even for a moment. It was simply a matter of an agreement I made with the prisoner priests—to find a subject which could realize on this Christmas Eve the greatest unanimity of Christians and nonbelievers." The literary merit of *Bariona* is surprising, given the utilitarian circumstances of its composition. Sartre's fears of readers' reactions seems to me unfounded. Granted the play acclaims the divinity of Christ and portrays a religious conversion, the essential message is conveyed under very thin symbolic disguises. The Christchild symbolizes the hope of liberation for the captive French; the freedom which his birth reveals to man is a Sartrean freedom *from* God, not salvation *in* God. If the priests took *Bariona* at face value, which seems unlikely,

[1] *Bariona* is contained in Contat and Rybalka, *Les Écrits de Sartre.*

they were duped as surely as were the prison authorities.

Bariona is set in Palestine on the eve of Jesus' birth. In two respects it anticipates *The Flies*: the traditional story is an allegory of a contemporary situation, and Sartre employs deliberate anachronism. Not only do the characters speak and act like twentieth-century men and women, but there are references to factories in Bethlehem, to the unemployed. The hero, Bariona, is the chief of a poverty-stricken village. Already chafing under the oppressive rule of the Romans, he is driven to despair by the announcement that the taxes will be raised still higher. Since any overt defiance of the Romans would bring total destruction on the village, he resolves that the villagers should pay the taxes for the sake of its living inhabitants. At the same time he tries to persuade the people that they should express both their despair and their revolt by refusing to allow the birth of any more children. Learning that his own wife has just discovered her pregnancy, he orders her to consult the sorcerers on methods of abortion.

It is at this point that the traditional events of Christmas Eve take place. In the middle of a night sweetly perfumed and strangely peaceful, an angel brings to shepherds the news of a newborn king in a manger. The angel sends a special message to Bariona: "Peace on earth to men of good will." But Bariona refuses to accept the angel's proclamation. Along with a cynical skepticism as to whether the sign is really from God, he is outraged by the counsel of peace and good will, which seems to him to command a sheeplike submission to oppression. "The good will of the poor who die without complaint at the doorsteps of the rich! The good will of the slave who is beaten and says Thank you! The good will of soldiers who are pushed to massacre and who fight without knowing why." [p. 599] Bariona prefers to rise up against Heaven, like a blasphemous column crying out the injustice done to men. If the message from the Eternal counsels submission, Bariona will refuse to listen. "For I am free; and against a free man God himself can do nothing." The appearance of the three Magi does not sway him. His suspicion that the Messiah will be the destruction of the Jews is confirmed when a soothsayer foretells Christ's mission of love and describes how he will consent to be led like a lamb to the slaughter. The legitimacy of Bariona's reaction is underscored by the fact that Sartre has already expressed in the words of a Roman official the idea that the Romans could make use of a Jewish Messiah who would work with them. Bariona finally resolves that for the sake of the Jews, he will visit this child and strangle him. Faced with the Nativity, he is unable to carry out his plan, partly because he does not find within himself enough hatred to kill the infant before the loving and hope-filled eyes of his parents. But his decision to accept and to serve Christ is made under the influence of Balthazar, one of the Oriental kings. Sartre himself played the role of Balthazar, and indeed he seems to be speaking in his own right, as the philosopher we have known.

In the first meeting with Bariona in his village, Balthazar had reproached him for giving way to the despair which arises when man is looked on as if he were pinned down in the present, like a scared animal or a stone. This is your despair, he says, "to chew the cud of the passing instant . . . to wrench your age away from the future and to encircle it with the present." But man is not like a stone. "The pebble does not hope, for it lives stupidly in a perpetual present. . . . Man is always much more than he is . . . he is always elsewhere." [pp. 604–5] Later when Bariona has decided not to kill the infant but is still unwilling to accept him, Balthazar explains Christ's true message. It is the good news that man is free. "Christ has come to teach you . . . that you are not your suffering. Whatever you do, and in whatever way you look upon it, you surpass it infinitely, for it is exactly what you wish it to be." Balthazar explains that Christ is man and so he will suffer. "But he is God, too, and with all his divinity he is beyond that suffering. And we others, men made in the image of God, we are beyond all our suffering exactly insofar as we resemble God." [pp. 624–25] Balthazar introduces a symbol which Sartre uses over and over in his later work, the free man's sense of somehow being without weight, of being "light" (*léger*). You are light and so is all that belongs to you, he tells Bariona. "The world and yourself, for you are to yourself a perpetually gratuitous gift."

In the simplest possible terms, Sartre has presented in this Christmas message the essence of the philosophical impact of *Being and Nothingness*, and Bariona understands the significance of the words much better than do most of Sartre's readers. He realizes that to accept what Balthazar offers means to be free, "free against God and for God, against myself and for myself." The individual is a self-making process. Suffering, or anything else which comes to him, is the material out of which a freedom makes itself. Every person finds himself within a situation already structured by other people and with the "coefficient of resistance" which is offered even by physical things. But the significance and meaning of whatever he encounters are created by him alone as he internalizes the situation and makes it his. This freedom is a dreadful freedom, as Marjorie Grene has called it, for it demands total responsibility without guarantee. Bariona illustrates Sartre's statement that once we admit human freedom, even if God exists nothing is changed. Man must still internalize what comes from God and decide for himself whether or not he will live "for God" or "for himself." We shall see that this idea remains true for Sartre even in the light of his own negative concept of the "missing God." (This nonexistent goal of human efforts is, Sartre claims, an unattainable ideal which serves as a driving force for each one of us—to be our own self-cause; that is, to exist as unrestricted freedom, surrounded by an absolute certainty that would justify our life and support its meaning.) In addition, Bariona sees that this freedom is both for and against himself. Sartrean freedom is not the progressive development of a given self with which one is born. To be oneself authentically is to make oneself spontaneously, not to burrow within until one discovers a true, innate form which *is* the self. Self-discovery is self-creation.

This radical ability of man to determine the quality of his life by the way he lives it is not intended to be limited to the free subjectivity by which the Stoic slave may so transcend his situation as to feel himself free while in chains. Its positive objective implications were immediately applicable to Sartre's fellow prisoners who watched the performance of *Bariona*. The message is a disguised appeal to revolt, to look on imprisonment as a period of preparation for action, not submission. As Orestes was to discover later in *The Flies*, once man knows he is free, neither gods nor tyrants can prevail. Moreover, the notion of freedom presented here does not belong exclusively to the period of *Being and Nothingness*. Sartre has spoken deprecatingly of the overoptimism of his early proclamations, but he has never renounced the essence of Balthazar's declaration. He continues to insist that even the most oppressive situation is individually internalized before it determines the objective behavior of the one who lives it. Here lies the germ of revolution. Revolt occurs, says Sartre, not when one is theoretically convinced of the injustice of an existing system but when one suddenly sees his life as demonstrating the impossibility of living. This theoretical conclusion from the *Critique* was literally the dramatic solution for Bariona. Immediately after he has resolved to accept Christ as Savior, Bariona learns that troops have been sent to hunt down the child and kill him (the "Slaughter of the Innocents"). Bariona sets forth with his followers, intending to engage the soldiers long enough to allow the Holy Family to escape. Knowing that he will die, Bariona bids his wife to raise their son without hiding from him the miseries of the world. And on the day when his son speaks of a bitter taste in his mouth, she must tell him, "Your father suffered all that you suffer and he died in joy." The note of rejoicing continues as Bariona concludes the drama by addressing the prison audience directly. "But I believe that for you too, on this day of Christmas, and on all other days—there will still be joy."

Was Sartre in bad faith when he showed Bariona recognizing his freedom with joy? Was he offering the prisoners a merely hollow consolation for the sake of improving morale? Did he at best seek to encourage revolt by sacrificing philosophical niceties? In *Being and Nothingness* we are told that freedom is revealed in anguish. Roquentin, in Sartre's first novel, *Nausea*, encountered freedom in nausea. Mathieu, the hero of *Les Chemins de la liberté* (*The Roads to Freedom*), realized despairingly that he was "free for nothing." Orestes, to be sure, declares in *The Flies*, "Human life begins on the far side of despair," but earlier in the play freedom was synonymous with exile and loneliness. It is not until *The Devil and the Good Lord* (*Le Diable et le Bon Dieu*, 1951) that we meet rejoicing like Bariona's. In this later play Goetz sheds tears of joy when he realizes that God is dead, and "there are only men." Granted the focus here is on atheism rather than psychological freedom per se, the intent is the same. Goetz has been searching for some sort of outside support for his action and embraces joyously the realization that to be without such guarantee is a liberation. It is only then that he feels capable of waging the war for men's political freedom. I think that there are two reasons for this variation in Sartre's treatment. First, we may note that Bariona and Goetz discover their freedom simultaneously with the opportunity for commitment in action. The recognition of psychological freedom can manifest itself immediately in acts against external forces which would deny or impede the scope of this freedom. In short, freedom is revolutionary. But freedom is double edged, and its negative aspect was of major concern to Sartre and his readers in the nineteen-thirties and -forties, particularly in the light of the religious and rational tradition which had dominated Western culture since the time of the pre-Socratic philosophers.

The counterpart to Bariona's joyous freedom for action is the metaphysical anguish experienced by Roquentin in *Nausea*.[2] We have noted that Sartre declared he "*was* Roquentin" but reproached himself for staying too aloof from his character.[3] I rather suspect that by

[2] *La Nausée* (Paris: Gallimard, 1938).

[3] Sartre discusses the relation between himself and his fictional hero in *Les Mots*, pp. 209–10, and in an interview, "Jean-Paul Sartre s'explique sur *Les Mots*," published in *Le Monde*, April 18, 1964.

this remark Sartre means three things: that Roquentin's overall attitude very much resembled his own at the time he wrote *Nausea*; that Roquentin's view of reality was, and still is, Sartre's own; but that Sartre at the age of fifty could not approve of what he had been at thirty and totally rejected Roquentin's (and his own earlier) solution to the problem of how to find personal meaning in a meaningless universe.

For our purpose the novel is important in that it presents, in the form of a private, emotional encounter, Sartre's ontological picture of reality, along with three possible responses to this sort of universe. The high point of the book is Roquentin's "horrible ecstasy" as he sits alone in a park and seems to see existence revealing itself. Sartre has deliberately couched his description of the episode in terms which suggest that it is the reverse image of the more familiar mystic experience. Instead of experiencing the presence of purifying Spirit, Roquentin senses the heavy weight of teeming matter, gobs of it surrounding him everywhere like pervading filth. Rather than grasping a transcendent unity in cosmic consciousness, Roquentin finds that "the diversity of things, their individuality, were only an appearance, a veneer. This veneer had melted, there remained only soft, monstrous masses, all in disorder— naked, in a frightful, obscene nakedness." [p. 162]

Roquentin does not say that all objects merge into one or that they are illusion in the sense of maya. The material does not manifest a higher immateriality. He tries to express two ideas about the surrounding world. One is that everything in it overflows the conventional forms and relations which we have imposed on it in our ordinary human ordering of reality. The root of the chestnut tree is both more and less than a root; perhaps we might best say that it is *other*. It is "below all explanation. Each of its qualities escaped it a little, flowed out of it, half solidified, became almost a thing; each one was *de trop*." This brings us to the second insight. When Roquentin says that every existent (including himself) is *de trop*, he means that it is absolutely contingent; that is, it is not necessary—it is there for nothing. When the Scholastics spoke of contingency, they meant that all things were dependent in their being—ultimately on God, of course. But for Roquentin contingency means absurdity, a total absence of relationship and meaning. Existence simply *is*; it does not mean anything. As an existent, Roquentin feels that he, too, is contingent, *de trop*, and he understands that this absurdity is the key to the nausea which swept over him from time to time. For he *was* nausea. By "nausea" Sartre refers specifically to the taste of oneself. If instead of seeking a conceptual answer to the question "What am I?" I try to *feel* my reality as an existent being, my self-awareness is likely to take the form of sheer visceral sensation.

What of consciousness in all this? Nausea reveals that one's consciousness is inextricably linked with a particular body, located in time and space. This is what Sartre calls its facticity. Yet consciousness cannot pin itself down or make itself an object for itself except in an infinite regress, "thinking about thinking about thinking. . . ." If my consciousness attempts to empty itself of all contents so as to be aware of itself only, it finds nothing there. As Roquentin stares in fascination at the chestnut root, he feels for an instant as if the chestnut root in its overpowering reality has absorbed him. He realizes that at this moment he is "nothing but an awareness of it."

Anyone familiar with the effects of mescaline will recognize that Roquentin's "horrible ecstasy" bears certain resemblances to the effects sometimes induced by that drug. Indeed, Sartre had lent himself as a subject to a psychiatrist friend who was doing some research with mescaline. Under its influence Sartre had the impression that objects around him kept transforming themselves into something else. In particular, the room seemed to be swarming with crabs and octopuses. For some time afterward he was bothered by the recurrence of such impressions to such an extent that he worried seriously lest he was losing his mind. They finally disappeared, to Sartre's great relief, after a particularly bad night in Venice when he confessed to Simone de Beauvoir that a lobster had been following him about for the entire evening.[4]

Even aside from the ecstasy in the park, *Nausea* retains suggestions of the mescaline experience. A hand suddenly seems to threaten to become a crab, a stone refuses to be a stone, purple suspenders suddenly are not purple. Yet Sartre, who in real life recognized that such transformations were not real except as events within his own psyche, and who worried for fear he was losing his sanity, did not intend to portray the workings of a sick mind in *Nausea*. One has the strong impression that the absurd universe described by the hero is a faithful picture of reality for the author. In actual fact, Roquentin's vision of a world which is without form or meaning or relation and of a consciousness which is nothing but an awareness of objects—together these comprise the ontological theory which led Sartre to present his philosophy under the title of *Being and Nothingness*.

[4] Simone de Beauvoir describes Sartre's experiences with mescaline in *La Force de l'âge*, pp. 216 ff.

Before turning at last to the philosophical formulation of the theory whose consequences we have seen in *Bariona* and in *Nausea*, we should look at three basic responses to the absurdity of the world as Sartre has portrayed them in his novel.

First, we may note that Roquentin, like Sartre in the thirties, shows no active concern with politics but displays a contemptuous, somewhat anarchistic, hatred of the bourgeoisie. The climax of Sartre's satiric sketch of provincial mores is Roquentin's visit to the local museum, where he contemplates the portraits of yesterday's leading citizens. In mock admiration he describes the self-confident stare of these pillars of society, men who spent their lives possessed with the idea of their right to exist and to all the special rights and privileges of existence.

No one of these men had died a bachelor, none of them died childless nor intestate, none without the last rites. Their life in order before God and the world, this day like every other day, they had slipped gently into death in order to lay claim to the share of eternal life which was their right. For they had a right to everything: to life, to work, to wealth, to authority, to respect and finally to immortality. [p. 109]

Transfixed by the judgment of the man in the portrait, Roquentin feels that his own right to exist is challenged. He cannot defend himself. "It was true . . . I did not have the right to exist. I had appeared by chance, I existed like a stone, a plant, a microbe. . . ." Looking within himself, he found no reassuring, ordered substance. At times his life "sent up vague signals, at other times only an inconsequential buzzing." Leaving the gallery, Roquentin says, "Farewell beautiful lilies, so finely arrayed in your little painted sanctuaries, farewell beautiful lilies, our pride and our reason for being. Farewell. Stinkers."

On the surface, this episode is brilliant if rather heavy-handed satire. But it is more than that. Implied in it is a central theme of Sartre's philosophy. Or, to put it another way, the satiric sketch portrays a form of individual bad faith and a society in bad faith. Essentially, bad faith is a lie to oneself which rests on the denial that a human being is a free self-making process. Its manifold structures are reducible to two basic forms; very often it exhibits a perpetual alternation from one to the other. I can acknowledge the inner realization of my freedom to the extent of feeling already beyond that "I" who performed a particular act in the past, and I can take advantage of this fact by disclaiming all responsibility for it. It is as though I should say that I am not a thief because I no longer feel as I did when I stole an object yesterday, or because I am unwilling to admit that my action has anything in common with the acts of those commonly called thieves. Or, conversely, I can deny myself as a free existent by assuming that both I and the world around me have been endowed with certain absolute and fixed qualities and values. It is in this second sense that the town's worthies are convinced of their natural rights and virtues. Contemporary social patterns and attitudes are supported by a God conceived precisely to uphold them. These citizens *are* their roles. They live in what Sartre calls the serious world, in which each action and every object has its clearly defined place and value assigned to it.

A second response, also in bad faith, is represented by the sentimental humanism of the Autodidacte or Self-taught Man, a stupid and pathetic individual who is educating himself by reading in alphabetical order all the books in the public library. Constantly reiterating his warm love for All Humanity, he in fact loves nobody. The sole concrete manifestation of his generalized love is a timid and furtive flirtation with homosexuality. The novel's attack on this species of false humanism and comparable forms was so violent that Sartre felt impelled to defend and explain himself in the popular lecture which first introduced many readers of English to Sartre's philosophy. Its French title states, "Existentialism Is a Humanism." Sartre explains in the lecture that atheistic existentialism is unreservedly and unabashedly a humanism insofar as it puts the whole burden of responsibility for human life squarely on the shoulders of man and of every individual man and woman. There are other kinds of humanism which Sartre opposes. He despises the so-called humanism by which each one would personally feel that he could take credit for the achievements of the great characters in history. Sartre refuses to ally himself with those who propose an abstract love of the idea of man, those who talk of undying human values and in their name sacrifice or exploit the lives of existing men and women. He also rejects any belief in an a priori human nature which would endow mankind with a given set of potentialities within which it will make its preoutlined history.

This last point has often been misunderstood. Naturally Sartre does not deny the existence of what we may call the human condition—our common biology, the fact that we exist finitely in time and space, our mortality. But he is unwilling to extend this list of givens to include innate psychological qualities of the sort implied in such old saws as "There will always be war (or class distinctions) because that's human nature." I think Sartre is right in arguing that the concept of a controlling human nature is most often used to explain man's failures or to restrict the possibilities of his future. This remains true even when it is disguised by the benevolent intentions of a B. F. Skinner. For to predefine the movement of freedom is to restrict it, to cut off forever a future which is truly open. For Sartre, the only truthful answer to a significant posing of the question "What is man?" is that he will have been what men and women together will have made him. Along with human nature, Sartre rejects such notions as the Jungian collective unconscious or a group consciousness which is a hyperorganism or metaphysical entity.

The humanism of the Self-taught Man and the serious world of the town's leaders are not so far apart as one might at first think. Both rest on the assumption that all of us share some sort of human essence, more fully realized in some individuals than in others but always serving to provide fixed criteria for judging. We shall see that in recent years Sartre has gone very far in the direction of claiming that the individual project is extricably intertwined with class and society. Yet even in the concept of the group-in-fusion, where Sartre claims that man's alienated otherness is finally healed, the union of many in one is accomplished outside, in the world, in a unity of common projects. Any merging of consciousnesses or notion of the group as a hyperorganism is firmly denied. Similarly, we should add that although Sartre has engaged his own freedom in a concrete political struggle for the rights of the oppressed, he has consistently avoided confusing these "rights" with the rights of the denizens of the portrait gallery; that is, Sartre has never claimed for any Marxist society, real or imagined, a nonhuman support, any more than he has sought to replace one ruling class by another. He has remained consistent with the point of view that since man is unjustifiable, since no Providence has designed either him or Society, any social structure and the value systems which reflect and support it must be considered as free creations which are left open to question. Sartre at present pleads for a total restructuring of society. Although apolitical, Roquentin's criticism of the stinkers was based on the same assumption: that all human enterprises are equally contingent.

Finally, what of Roquentin's own solution? I suspect that at the time Sartre wrote *Nausea*, he would have held that his hero's solution, however contingent, was at least in good faith. It was, in fact, identical with the author's own. But it was not a resolution which Sartre was willing to accept for very long.

The revelation which Roquentin witnessed in the "horrible ecstasy" was of existence. Within the novel, "existence" becomes synonymous with "absurdity," but it is contrasted with "being." There are certain human creations—such as a detective story, a song, or a mathematician's circle—which are not absurd. Neither do they exist. Instead, they have being—or, more precisely, they possess reason for being. Roquentin says that "the circle is sufficiently explained by the rotation of a segment of a straight line around one of its extremities" (p. 164). Each of its parts has its *raison d'être* in the whole. A novel or a song rises up independent of the pages or record on which it is inscribed. It exists absolutely—a whole made up of parts, each one of which is significantly explained and supported by it. In contrast, Roquentin's life contained none of these perfect, formed "adventures." There was nothing either within or outside of it which made it necessary, explained it, provided a reason for being. He was simply there, and the acts which he was free to perform had no meaning except that which he decided to bestow on them. In other words, Roquentin experienced freedom, in anguish and in nausea, as pure contingency. But what he yearned to do was to use this freedom in such a way as to achieve within his own life some of the perfect being of the circle.

At the end of the novel he finds a solution which partially, not entirely, achieves this goal. The thought comes to him while he is sitting in a café, listening to a recording of a popular song. (A much wiser choice on Sartre's part than Beethoven, for example, who might have lent an aura of nobility or sanctity to the occasion.) Across the melody, Roquentin tries to imagine the composer and the singer.

There they are—two who have been saved. Perhaps they believed up to the very end that they were drowned in existence. And yet nobody could think of me as I think of them with such gentleness. . . . For me they are a little like the dead, a little like the heroes of a novel; they have cleansed themselves of the sin of existing. Not completely, of course —but as much as any man can.

In his imagination Roquentin sees himself writing a novel, a book which will someday lead its readers to think of him as he thinks now of the composer and the singer. He, too, will be able to look on this completed being which he has made, and it will shed a redeeming light over his own past. Recollecting the moment when he first decided to write the novel, he will see the same kind of necessary connections one sees in the unfolding of an adventure in a detective story. "I would feel my heart beat faster and would say to myself, 'It was on that day, at that hour, that it all started.' And I should succeed—at least in the past, only in the past, in accepting myself."

Inasmuch as the novel about to be written is obviously *Nausea,* one might be tempted to classify it as simply one more of the autobiographical first works in which an author shows how he found himself as a writer. In truth, the conclusion is hardly original. Even Plato's *Symposium* described how our longing for eternity may be partly assuaged by creating "children of the mind." Later Sartre criticized himself explicitly for having tried to find in literature a means of salvation. Already by the time of *Bariona,* he had abandoned the posture of nonengagement. But to dismiss the novel as nothing more than the writer's first self-realization would be to ignore all the metaphysical implications which have preceded and to miss the fact that the solution is not exclusively or even primarily personal and psychological but philosophical. In finding a way to approximate the union of being and existence, Roquentin serves to demonstrate Sartre's thesis that everyone tries in his own way to effect the impossible union of Being-in-itself and Being-for-itself. It is to try to realize the "missing God." This idea Sartre has never renounced even though to maintain it is to view human existence as being in a certain respect a failure, to make man a "useless passion." If we look at the form of Roquentin's solution rather than its specific content, I think it remains as valid for Sartre's projects today as it was for him in the late thirties. Yet I do not believe that to make this statement is to accuse him of being a philosopher of despair. All of this will be much clearer if we look now at the fundamental ontology of *Being and Nothingness,* at Sartre's analysis of the nature of Being and of Human Being.

3

THE USELESS PASSION

Conscious human being is Being-for-itself. The rest is Being-in-itself. The latter has priority, for consciousness could not exist without something to be conscious *of*. But there is no reciprocity. Being-for-itself needs Being-in-itself in order to exist, but the In-itself does not need the For-itself. No wonder Sartre has stated that his philosophy is simply the attempt to work out the consequences of a coherent atheism. Being-for-itself, the being of consciousness, is nothing at all in itself. For it is not in itself. It is nothing but the perpetual process of setting up a relation with Being, of focusing on Being in a particular way, of taking a point of view on it. But this Being on which consciousness is dependent has neither meaning nor form nor significance except as it is "worked on" by consciousness. In itself it is simply undifferentiated fullness. Sartre declares that his existentialism is the most thoroughgoing atheism the world has known, for it holds that all order and unity and rationality have been brought into the world by human consciousness and do not exist without it.

At first thought this view of reality may appear to be both idealist and nonscientific. But let us look a little more closely. It is not idealism. Consciousness does not create its objects in the sense of making them exist. Indeed, we may say that the existence of consciousness depends on something outside itself, for it exists only as awareness *of* objects. Solipsism is not a problem for

Sartre, for consciousness is never shut up inside itself. It is always outside in the world; it exists as a process of setting up a relation with Being. Consciousness depends, in its being, on something which is not consciousness. Yet this theory is no naïve realism either. Consciousness is pure activity. All inertness is on the side of Being-in-itself. Sartre has said that Being is the condition for all revealing. But without consciousness, Being remains unrevealed. "Revealing," for Sartre, is more than uncovering or unveiling. To reveal involves organizing, developing, shaping—in short, working over.

It turns out that Being-in-itself is, so to speak, the raw material out of which consciousness selects, places, arranges its objects. But we must be careful. It would not be correct to interpret Sartre as if he were presenting in new form the old Aristotelian idea of a formless material substance which lies beneath and supports all qualities. Nor is he a Neo-Kantian; he does not postulate any thing-in-itself, or noumenal reality which Being really is, apart from its appearances. Neither must we fall into the temptation of imposing on this Being-in-itself a Neoplatonic or Oriental interpretation, one which would see in the activity of consciousness something equivalent to inscribing, on an eternal, nonmaterial oneness, a half-illusory world of maya. Sartre remains firmly a phenomenologist, a designation which at one point he explicitly preferred to existentialist. Being is nothing more than its appearances; it is never either more or other than it appears to be. When Sartre says that Being is also transphenomenal, he does not mean that it has an ultimate reality which is inapprehensible by us but simply that Being is not exhausted by its appearances. In other words, Being *is*, whether it is revealed by consciousness or not. Consciousness is what is contingent. There is no necessity for Being to be revealed, but consciousness can exist only as it reveals Being.

In a way it is futile to ask what Being is apart from our consciousness of it, for the very posing of the question asks what Being is for the one who asks it. Sartre is quite aware of this. In fact, he has said even apropos of matter that we never encounter it in a pure state except abstractly. But in the same way we can ask abstractly about Being-in-itself, and to this question Sartre gives a succinct answer. All that we can say of Being-in-itself is that it is. If we were to go so far as to say, "Being is there," or even, "There is Being," we would already have introduced the point of view which belongs to consciousness. Being is itself, with no gap or emptiness or lack or need or meaning or differentiation. At the same time Sartre speaks of this outside "stuff" as possessing a "coefficient of resistance." One cannot do whatever one likes with Being. And it is all too obvious that things in the world about whose existence I am totally unaware can deviate and impede my projects— as, for example, when I stumble over a stone in a dark wood. Obviously further explanation is necessary.

Let us consider further, using some of Sartre's examples and choosing others from universal everyday experience, moving from what is most apparent in our own encounter with the real to what is most controversial. I hope that in this way we may avoid concluding either that Sartre is belaboring the obvious or that he seeks to impose on us an idealist mystification.

It is easy to see that we bestow a particular significance on otherwise neutral objects when we subject them to our human projects. The willow branch contains the form of a switch or of a whistle only if I put it there. The mountain is an impediment or an instrument depending on whether I want to be on the other side of it or to secure a view of the surrounding landscape or to prove my physical dexterity by climbing it. The flowers which cover its sides are neutralized as an ignored part of the background, or are appreciated aesthetically, or are viewed as objects for botanical study. Sartre, of course, goes much farther than this. Not only does consciousness introduce significance, meaning, and purpose, but neither destruction nor growth nor change nor becoming occurs in the In-itself without the presence of consciousness. But, someone will say, surely this is nonsense. Geology and developmental biology exist, after all, and these sciences are based on the fact that man can demonstrably study and describe the processes which took place before his own emergence. We must note immediately that this description presumes that in some way consciousness is present to that prehuman past. It reveals this past, and Sartre would say that in a certain sense the evolutionary process did not exist until or before this revelation by consciousness. Indeed, the very concepts of "until" and "before" are possible only in the presence of consciousness.

Sartre's comments on potentiality may help to clarify things. Heavy, leaden clouds are said to "promise" rain. Put less anthropomorphically, the clouds hold the potentiality of rain. Neither Sartre nor anyone else would deny that the physical makeup of the sky is different at this moment from what it would be if we said, "There is no sign of rain today." Yet strictly speaking, the *potentiality* of rain exists only by virtue of a witnessing subject who can place an imaginary—i.e., nonexisting or not yet existing—future side by side with the present state of the sky. The clouds with their heavy blackness will literally no longer exist in that problematic future when there is rain instead. There will simply be a different physical configuration in the sky. The promise of rain, the potentiality, cannot exist without reference to time, and time is introduced by the conscious observer.

Here we meet Sartre's famous concept of "nihilation." The term is as much a neologism in French as in English: *néantisation*, nihilation; *néantir*, to nihilate. These words are related, of course, to the even better known *néant*, nothingness, which similarly did not exist in French until Sartre established it in philosophical terminology. Much misunderstanding could have been avoided, at least in English-speaking countries, if would-be interpreters of Sartre had not yielded to the fatal temptation to make the terms equivalent to annihilation. Obviously the clouds are not destroyed by consciousness. Even as objects of perception they are not annihilated. Consciousness continues to see the clouds even as mentally it nihilates them. What happens is that consciousness in imagination cancels out the present cloud formation. Actually, there is a double nihilation. Employing Sartre's own metaphor, we may say that consciousness wraps the present clouds in a muff or shell of Nothingness and sets up in its place an imagined—that is, nonreal—state of affairs in which rain has replaced the clouds. So where are potentialities? They are in the clouds, but they are put there, made to emerge by a consciousness. Similarly, the prehistoric glaciers, the rising or sinking of mountains, all destructions and emergences are at best only shifting masses of being until consciousness has come to place one state beside another, imposing form, significance, differentiation.

Looked at in this way, Sartre's view of Being-in-itself may seem almost disappointingly obvious. Indeed, it bears some resemblance to the common-sense solution to the old question of whether there is any sound when the tree falls unheard in a deep forest: the vibrations in the air are certainly there, but sound as such does not exist until it has struck an eardrum. I myself believe that this side of Sartre's theory of being is less revolutionary than the other—his notion of consciousness. Still we should not underestimate its consequences. In the first place, it is sternly nonteleological. Being-in-itself is not there *for* anything. It is absolutely impersonal. By itself it provides neither meaning nor unity. The scientific world reflects one kind of human ordering. The world of the cubist painter is another. And like all phenomenologists, Sartre distinguishes between the scientific and the life world. The latter, with its emotional colorings, its personal linkings of cause and effect, is different for each individual. But this private world of each one of us, in which the individual consciousness remains the center of reference, is the world which is absolutely valid and inescapable for the one who lives it. Thus, even if we try to speak abstractly of what Being is in itself, we are constantly referred to the Being which reveals this world to us—that is, to Being-for-itself.

In spite of the fact that Sartre uses the term hundreds of times in *Being and Nothingness* and describes it over and over in various aspects and approaches, Being-for-itself is not easy to define precisely. Probably we are safest in saying that it is conscious Being. But immediately we encounter a problem. Whenever Sartre uses the word consciousness (*conscience*), he clearly means human consciousness. Most of us assume that inorganic matter and plants are not conscious, but animals definitely are conscious. Yet Sartre's description of the For-itself is not applicable to even the most highly evolved nonhuman animals. Although, to my knowledge, he has never clarified the position of animals in his system, it seems plain that they must fall on the side of Being-in-itself. I myself do not feel totally satisfied with this solution, for it seems to me that there is more of intention and purpose in animal life than Sartre allows for the In-itself. Perhaps the truth is that Sartre is simply not interested in animals and has not bothered to consider them as a special case needing explanation. At any rate, we may easily see why, for him, animals would be closer to nonconscious nature than to human consciousness. The animal, so far as we can tell, is not free to stand apart and question his situation. He has no consciousness of self, and that is the essential distinction.

To be correct, then, we should say that the For-itself is self-conscious, reflective Being. Is Being-for-itself synonymous with consciousness? On numerous occasions Sartre uses the two terms as if they were interchangeable. In strict accuracy, I think we should conclude that the two are inseparable but not the same. We might perhaps say that the For-itself is embodied consciousness, but we must quickly add that consciousness and body are not two separate entities as in the old mind-body dualism. To speak of consciousness as separate, even conceptually, from the body would be like severing digestion from the digestive organs. The comparison is fairly apt, for just as digestion is not the stomach, liver, intestines, and so forth, so it is nothing apart from them. The body may in death exist without consciousness, but at this point there is no longer Being-for-itself. Consciousness is not an entity but active process. If we say that Being-for-itself *has* consciousness, this does not mean that it possesses consciousness, like holding onto an object, but that it is characterized by being conscious.

Sartre's concept of consciousness rests on three principles: consciousness is always consciousness *of* something; every consciousness is self-consciousness; and both of these statements are possible and explainable by the fact that by virtue of consciousness the For-itself introduces a Nothingness into Being.

If I am conscious of an object, simultaneously I am implicitly conscious of not being that object. In other words, my very awareness of an object includes a non-reflective realization that the awareness and the object of the awareness are not the same. That consciousness cannot exist independently of any object is neither a difficult concept nor an entirely new one. We may note a parallel—more precisely, a concrete application—by reference to any one of the senses. There is no sight or smell, no touching, tasting, or hearing without something which is seen, smelled, touched, tasted, or heard; this is true whether the object is out there in the world or in the body. William James described consciousness as a process of attending to or focusing on objects, picking them out of the big booming, buzzing confusion which constantly surrounds us. Phenomenologists before Sartre had spoken of intending rather than attending to objects: the intending consciousness is again always *of* something. Sartre's originality lies in his notion that all consciousness is self-consciousness but that this self is not identical with the personal ego.

It seems to me that appeal to experience bears out Sartre's claim that perception of an object includes the recognition that the object perceived is not the same as the perceiving or the perceiver. To be aware of something involves a placing of it as *there* in relation to the awareness which so places it. Up to a point this is clear and easy. To smell a skunk is quite obviously not to be the skunk or the scent which the skunk has emitted. Even visceral self-awareness or that nauseous taste of oneself which Sartre so effectively described in *Nausea* is the object of consciousness—or at least consciousness-aware-of-an-object—rather than consciousness itself. If we grant that some background awareness of the body is as necessary to any conscious act as a physical background is to the perception of a material object, still this is not to claim that the taste or the matter is *in* consciousness, either as a necessary ingredient or as a primary structure. Sartre, of course, would add that nothing can be *in* consciousness, for consciousness, being neither place nor entity, has no inside and no contents.

But then what is this self which Sartre has in mind when he says that all human consciousness is self-consciousness? It is certainly not the biographical self with its accumulation of memories and plans for the future. Nor is it the object of reflection as when I "think of myself," whether in introspective self-questioning (which inevitably involves some degree of appraisal of the past) or in observation of myself in action. This second sort of awareness of self may actually impede free activity, as when my awkward "self-consciousness" prevents graceful dancing or an easy flow of social chatter. What happens here is that the real object of intention becomes not the original activity but myself as performer, and the distraction of thought prevents the accomplishment of its original aim. On other occasions the self-in-action appears to be an essential element of the object of consciousness; for example, when a salesman is aware that he is making an effective sales pitch and is stimulated

to greater efforts. In neither case is the object of reflection identical with the self-consciousness which Sartre
identifies with consciousness itself. The self in our examples is directly the object *of* consciousness as much as
the tree is an object *of* perception. We are dealing with
a reflective consciousness, but the original consciousness,
for Sartre, is prereflective. There are innumerable occasions when we are not directly thinking about ourselves.
I may be so caught up in a suspense film that I cry
out in alarm when danger threatens a character who is
emphatically not identical with me as I sit safely in the
theater. In any absorbing activity and in thousands of
insignificant perceptions, the awareness contains no sign
of my personal self.

Since I can thus put my autobiographical self in
parentheses temporarily, we must ask further what is the
self which is always present in consciousness even when
—at least on the reflective level—I am not self-centered.
Sartre's answer may at first seem to be a barren abstraction so devoid from all connection with everyday experience as to be meaningless or at least unprofitable.
The self which makes all consciousness a self-consciousness is only that inseparable aspect of consciousness by
which to be aware is to be aware that the object of
consciousness is not consciousness; thus, consciousness
includes a reference to itself as consciousness. Sartre uses
parentheses as a visual device to distinguish between
reflective consciousness *of* self, *conscience de soi*, and
prereflective self-consciousness, *conscience (de) soi*. Actually the latter is always present. Even in my deepest
introspection the consciousness which directs the self-
reflection is itself a self-consciousness.

In its original and basic structure, consciousness,
while it is individual and particular, is nonpersonal. Be-

fore jumping to the conclusion that such a position contradicts common sense, let us consider whether it does not in fact serve to explain that sense of bewildered frustration which inevitably accompanies any serious attempt to pin down and know the self. Experientially I tend to interpret my difficulty in deciding exactly who or what "I" am as deriving from a gap between the "I" and the "Me." I am all too aware that whether it is a matter of judging myself or of making a decision as to what will be best for me, the "I" cannot be counted on for either neutrality or stability. At such moments I may take recourse in scrutinizing the "Me" more closely, as if I could find there some clear guarantee and support for the validity of the particular "I" which is in process of deciding; that is, to identify it as being my true and deepest self. Yet I feel obscurely that no such scrutiny, however thorough, can ever reveal or release that hidden "I."

The failure stems from two causes. First, there is an obvious contradiction in my very attempt. I want to make that evanescent "I" stand before me so that I can grasp its qualities objectively; that is, turn it into an object. But an object for whom? Not for the object "Me." It can only be for another subject "I" in an infinite regress or, at best, a game of mirrors. So far we have not progressed beyond Kant. We have simply reaffirmed him. My second mistake, according to Sartre, is one which I share with many distinguished philosophers and psychologists. I am wrong in thinking that what I call my consciousness is to be identified, even ideally, with any "I" or that it is personal. No matter what intricacy of personality structures may emerge under my own introspective scrutiny or in psychoanalysis, these drives, tendencies, qualities, and habits form part of the accumulated experiential data of consciousness but are not part of its original structure. They are objects of consciousness, and Sartre puts them on the side of Being-in-itself.

Let us turn again to what happens in my introspection. If I probe inward to find out what I really am, the only demonstrable objective unity I can discover is inextricably bound up with my autobiography. Yet I feel that this accumulated essence is too inert to be that directing consciousness which projects itself toward the future. I sense confusedly that the subject consciousness cannot be identified with any given set of attitudes; yet I remain convinced that throughout my psychic experience there is some transcendent unity, something which is involved in every state of consciousness without being restricted to any one of them. This mystery is explained by Sartre's conclusion that each consciousness is particular but not personal. The personal ego is on the side of the psychic; that is, it belongs with all the psychological phenomena which we view objectively as the personality. But the personality is not a structure of consciousness in the sense that we might describe the makeup of an optical lens. It is that at which the lens is directed. Consciousness itself is not timid or courageous or avaricious or generous. These qualities exist *for* consciousness. It evokes them, brings them into the world, for others and for itself.

Reference to time may help us at this point. If I see a form approaching, I may react to it with an immediate impulse of fear or aversion. At that instant the fear or aversion is as much a part of the perception as the particular angle of my vision is. The following moment I may reflect back on the reaction. Now the fear or aversion is the object of consciousness, and it depends on a new act of consciousness to reaffirm it or to judge it mistaken. The emotion clearly represents a possible choice for consciousness rather than a fixed integral part of its structure. But what of the sense of I-ness and my-ness? Sartre insists that these manifestations of the "I" and "me"—that is, of the ego—derive from a unification of experience after-the-event. The unity of my psychic life lies precisely in my accumulation of psychic experience. The "I" and the "Me" are respectively the active and passive ideal poles of all that I have experienced and will experience. Therefore, the feeling of frustration which comes over me when I try introspectively to find myself reflects exactly what I actually am. If I seek to find an "I" endowed with personal qualities, I can find one objectively in my psychic history, but the "I" is always in the past or, by imagination, in the future. The consciousness which continues to produce it is without personal qualities. Thus my dim comprehension that the active source of my awareness transcends any "I" which even the most accurate self-analysis could evoke is exactly correct.

If consciousness stands aloof even from the personality, it is determined by nothing save itself. Here is the source of Sartre's radical freedom. My consciousness is not myself. The self exists in only two ways: it is the ideal essence of my past, and it is the never realized ideal of the future which my consciousness projects. I do not exist as a bundle of potentialities and determined traits. Consciousness *pursues* a self; consciousness is a self-making process, a self-projection which is never completed so long as consciousness exists. The neurotic who seeks so anxiously to identify his real self asks the wrong question; he should inquire, rather, what self he wishes to create.

I do not deny that there are difficulties in Sartre's position. Two are particularly pressing. First, why are the feelings of I-ness and my-ness so strong if consciousness is at heart impersonal? How can we account for the sense of unity in immediate conscious experience? This problem strikes me as not insurmountable. Whatever else we may say about consciousness, it is evidently a function attached to a particular body. Thus each consciousness is individualized, though to say that consciousness is individual is not the same as saying that it is personal. The fact that a specific body is always there as a background for every conscious act is enough in itself to provide the necessary unity and the distinction from other consciousnesses. Continuity, I-ness and my-ness derive from the fact that, for a consciousness, all its earlier awarenesses remain as actual or potential objects for consciousness within the order which it has itself imposed. I believe that the intimate personal sense of being bound up with an inseparable ego occurs precisely at those times when we do reflect on our selves. If I am nonreflectively engaged in an activity, the coherence of my thoughts is likely to be provided by the objects with which I am working; that is, it emerges like the potentiality in the clouds which we saw revealed by the activity of consciousness in the world. It is because the "I" and "Me" are found only in reflection that I feel forever I am in some way a stranger to myself. Another way of putting this is to state that I am always aware of a separation between awareness and the object of awareness even when I try to make myself that object.

Granted that this self-consciousness is impersonal, what *is* it? This is the second and much more difficult problem. Even if we are to say that the self of self-consciousness is not personal, it seems that it must be something or there could be no sense of self. Or if consciousness is process and not entity, of what is it a process? I am not sure that Sartre could—or would—claim that he could give a totally satisfactory answer to that basic question. This is partly because to do so would involve us in purely metaphysical speculations which seek to go behind reality itself. It is as though the Christian should express his discontent with the statement that God is eternal reality and truth and ask, "But why is God?" Sartre claims that his ontology is a *description* of man's Being-in-the-world, not a speculation as to how what is came to be. Sartre does not claim to describe what consciousness is, in this absolute sense, any more than the psychologist does when he says that thought is an electrochemical reaction; nor does the physicist explain what energy really *is* when he describes it as electrons, protons, and so on. Nevertheless, Sartre claims to be giving an ontology, or description of reality, and it seems that in this limited sense, at least, he must tell us not only what consciousness does but what it is.

One thing is clear. Consciousness is not Being. Some readers jump quickly to the conclusion (and Sartre admittedly gives them some justification) that consciousness *is* simply Nothing—or at most Nothingness—but whether there is any real distinction between Nothingness and Nothing remains obscure. Actually, this is not what Sartre has said. Sartre does hold that the difference between Being-in-itself and Being-for-itself is precisely Nothing. It is man, as Being-for-itself, who brings Nothing into the world. Consciousness is the process of introducing this Nothingness. It makes Nothingness *be*. To create a Nothingness is to make something happen. If I put a crack in a uniform surface, there are new form and pattern and dimension. We cannot answer the question as to why suddenly there was Being-for-itself. All we can say is that Being-for-itself is distinct from Being-in-itself exactly insofar as it is able to effect this psychic withdrawal from the rest of Being, that it introduces into all of Being, including itself, this gap or Nothingness which makes possible the tremendous process of questioning, establishing differentiation, meaning, purpose—in short, self-conscious psychic life. Being-for-itself is conscious Being; that is, it possesses consciousness but only in the way that the body "has" digestion. Just as digestion is a making but not a maker, so consciousness is a process of evoking awareness of objects. To be aware of an object is to be aware that an object is outside of the center of awareness and not the same as the center of awareness. This center is never made explicit. We may conclude that the process itself is the center. We may, if we prefer, go back to the brain which initiated the process. Still the process is not the brain cell, nor is the brain aware of itself as brain. Consciousness is awareness of itself as awareness at the same time that it is aware of its object. Beyond that we cannot go.

But we have gone far enough to glimpse the tremendous consequences of consciousness thus conceived. On the positive side, each person is seen as a spontaneous, free upsurge, a self-creating process which deals with its own psychic material in the same way it deals with objects out there in the world; that is, it objectifies them in its present choice and constitutes them as background data for all future choices. Consciousness lives within a world which it has structured in the light of an original attitude or orientation which Sartre calls the "choice of being." This, for Sartre, replaces the primary structures or irreducible ultimates of traditional psychology—for example, Freud's three stages of sexuality, the Oedipus complex, or Alfred Adler's "will to power." It is different from all of them in two important respects: first, the nature of the choice is unique for every individual, for it is in fact a *choice*; second, consciousness is aware that even this most fundamental of all orientations is not irrevocable. In a fashion reminiscent of the religious doctrine of sudden conversion, Sartre argues that consciousness may in fact literally evoke the birth of a new personality by choosing a new way of relating itself to Being. To choose a new set of responses to Being is to choose a new self. We can see how for Bariona the revelation of such radical freedom came as a liberation and occasion for joy. Suppose he had lived on. Would the joy have endured? Would his choice of Being, translated into concrete action, have continued to seem to him the only one commensurate with the revelation? Sartre argues that at every moment we are uneasily aware that our choice of Being, no matter what it is, could be revoked and replaced. This hidden awareness is the source of anguish and the price we pay for freedom. Psychologically, the *instant* is neither the passing moment nor an abstract point by which to measure time. The instant is the ever-present threat that no choice of Being is final or supported by anything save the consciousness which continues to choose it.

In recent years Sartre has introduced certain modifications into his description of the way in which we choose our Being. He has never renounced the view that each person internalizes, structures, and determines the meaning, for him, of whatever situation he encounters or is born into. Lately Sartre writes far less of individual radical conversion and gives more weight to all the factors which make it a rarity in most persons' experience. Yet I think that there is a definite link be-

tween this emphasis on the instant as a total rupture
in lived time and Sartre's doctrine of social revolution.
It is significant that in stating the aims of revolution,
he has always advocated a total resocialization, a complete restructuring of society and its value systems—to
such a degree, indeed, that even at the period when he
was closest to Marxism, Sartre spoke of the emergence
of a society which would be characterized by a philosophy of freedom beyond Marxism. In this idea of continued self-transcendence, Sartre remains consistent in
seeing freedom as being without guarantees.

What most men and women would find convenient,
of course, would be the ability to know that one is
absolutely free to make of life what one wishes while
at the same time possessing an absolute criterion for
what we ought to wish. In other words, we want the
freedom of being able to choose without having that
choice determined by anything, not even by God, but
we should like to have some external support for this
freedom, to give it repose and security. We yearn to
have the absoluteness of Being-in-itself, which simply *is*,
and at the same time the freedom of the For-itself,
which can choose to be one thing rather than another.
This desire to be at once a Being-in-itself-for-itself is
not to wish that we might find an existing God outside
ourselves. It is the desire to *be* God. Sartre claims that
all of us live as if this impossible goal must be pursued
even though it is not attainable. Man tries to deny himself as man in order, by becoming God, to make God
exist. But God does not exist, and man's sacrifice is in
vain. "Man is a useless passion."

Sartre says of human consciousness that it drags its past behind it like a mermaid with her tail. The image is apt in its very incongruity and expresses quite effectively one of the paradoxes of human reality: past and present are blended in a single being, yet there is a transformation, a change of nature as present experience becomes past. The For-itself "is completed behind itself as a thing in the world." [1] Being-for-itself becomes, in the past, Being-in-itself. Yet the past does not cease to belong to the present For-itself any more than the mermaid's tail is severed from the rest of her body. The mermaid *is* her tail as well as her head, though the change of nature is clearly discernible. But if we acknowledge the validity of the metaphor, have we not fallen into a difficulty? Have we not established that the human person is both Being-in-itself and Being-for-itself, which Sartre explicitly denies? If we forget that consciousness is process and not entity, this is exactly what we have done. But let us look more closely at Sartre's concept of temporality.

We can easily conceive of time as the simple human ordering of external changes and succession of events. So far as the "time of the world" is concerned, Sartre's explanation of temporality is not essentially different from his discussion of destruction, potentiality, and the

[1] *Being and Nothingness*, translated by Hazel E. Barnes (New York: Philosophical Library, 1956), pp. 146–47.

like. By virtue of its power of nihilation, the For-itself introduces the "before" and "after" into existence. Time is much more than this. To say that the For-itself is temporal is the same as to say that it exists. To exist as human is to make oneself be in time. Being-for-itself exists in "three temporal ekstases." Sartre uses the word "ekstases" without mystic overtones, of course, but with the literal meaning it has held since it was first used in Greek philosophy: a standing apart from or outside (oneself). Consciousness (in the present) is not what it is (past) and is what it is not (future). The same psychic distance which consciousness places between itself and any other object stands between the present For-itself and its past experiences and, again, between itself and its projected future. I have to be my past in the mode of not-being it, says Sartre; that is, I assume a point of view on my past, subjecting it perpetually to new judgment. We may say that the past was what it was; that is like saying that the stone is a stone. There is also a sense in which we can ask what the past *is*. This is to ask about the meaning of the past, something which is forever in question. In short, the Past is Being-in-itself; the For-itself determines the significance of its Past. I decide it by my present choice just as I decree that a rock is an obstacle or an adornment for a garden according to my current project.

We must quickly note, however, that to speak of a project, even though we correctly designate it as a present project, is not to limit it to the present. Sartre interprets "present" as inextricably associated with "presence." In the present I am a presence to an object or a situation which my consciousness internalizes and objectifies. But this attention on my part is always *for* something, which means that it is *toward* something.

A project is a self-projection toward. I reach for an orange in order to peel and to eat it. I take a step in order to open the door in order to. . . . Even my idle perusal of the landscape while my thoughts are elsewhere is to fill in time, to give me something to do. What determines the meaning which I give to the past is the kind of future which I am in the process of proposing or purposing for myself. "My past comes to meet me out of the future," Sartre says, borrowing from Heidegger.

Of course there is also a psychic distance between my present consciousness and the future goal which I envision. We saw that I have to be my past by not-being it—that is, by choosing its relation to my present consciousness. Comparably but conversely, I am the future which is not yet inasmuch as my present existence is characterized by the attempt to bring that future into being. Qualitatively if not legally, the man who stole yesterday and blames himself for the fact *is* not a thief even though he *was* a thief. The man who plans to steal tomorrow has already chosen himself as a thief, though only the act itself will so define him in that future present. Anguish may overwhelm me as I confront any one of the temporal dimensions. I am anguished by the sudden realization that the resolution I made yesterday, that "unalterable decision," is powerless to determine my present conduct unless I remake it as a living choice. The resolution is back there in the past at a distance from me. It depends on me to summon it now or to leave it there forever. In anguish I realize, particularly at moments of crisis, that *nothing* prevents me from performing an act which would have the effect of cutting me off from my past completely. It is with anguish that I plan a future for myself and then wonder how it will be lived by that future consciousness which will show up to keep the rendezvous which "I" have made for it.

Let us return to Sartre's statement that I have to be my past in the mode of not being it. So far we have considered only the free subjectivity involved in my not being my past but rather choosing it and remaking it. But there is another aspect. Even if I view my past as an object, I still *have to be it*. Sartre points out that though consciousness exists as a free spontaneity, it cannot exist—even spontaneously—without having to temporalize itself. The temporality of consciousness is inseparable from its freedom, but it is by virtue of being temporal that consciousness finds itself confronted with necessity. The Being of the For-itself is contingent; but once it exists, it cannot choose not to have been born. It cannot choose not to be free, though it may in bad faith try to ignore that freedom. It cannot avoid having to make itself by a continuous process of choosing. To refuse to choose is already to have chosen. Sartre has said, rather poetically, that with each act I inscribe my Being in the world. My objectified self is the accumulation of the things which I have done; it is imaged in the external world, which has been altered by my presence to it. In this sense we find Sartre's emphasis wholly on the objective side. The person who dreams of writing a great novel is not a novelist until he has written it. Sartre has no use for the "mute inglorious Milton." "You *are* your life," Inez tells Garcin in *No Exit*. The human person is both Being and Nothingness. Lived time is a process of objectification, of reification, of constituting a part of one's being into a thing, of becoming—like the mermaid—a hybrid.

The inseparability of freedom and responsibility holds as strongly for the past as for the future. If I am

free, I am responsible. This point has often been misunderstood by readers of Sartre who feel that without
God or a personalized cosmic Being, there is nobody
and nothing for me to be responsible to. Responsibility
is often understood in the sense of having to give an
account of oneself for what one has done, and it is
subtly implied that there is some sort of higher judge
to serve as arbiter. Within Sartre's philosophy, there is
certainly neither deity nor person nor any existing objective ideal to serve as final reference point or criterion.
Yet I am responsible, both responsible *to* and responsible
for. I am responsible *for* whatever actions I have performed inasmuch as I am the author of them. I am
responsible for my past because I have made it what it
was and because I bestow on it its meaning in my
present. I am responsible for my future because I am
the author of the acts which will make it what it will be.
We may say that I account for my life in every choice
I make, for the nature of the choice is decided exactly
by the way in which I do account for my past and
choose my future. To whom am I accountable? To
everyone and to myself. Although I may not acknowledge the accuracy of others' judgments, I cannot keep
them from judging me. I cannot remain ignorant that
others have judged me and will continue to judge me.
Nor can I prevent their judgments from becoming part
of the data which I have at my disposal as I appraise
myself. For I have an outside. My consciousness exists
as an awareness of something outside itself. My acts
are out there in the world. The world has been affected
by what I have done. My past is *my* Being-in-itself. I
cannot avoid taking a point of view on it any more
than I can avoid seeing the street in which I look for
my friend. I must account for it to myself, for it *has*

been myself. It is my responsibility, but it cannot be my refuge. For it is In-itself, and I *am* myself only as a pursuit of self. Essence is the past; existence is freedom. The past is Being; the present is a wrenching away from Being.

The longing for self-coincidence is not really different from the desire to be God. It is significant that even in religious traditions which are not pantheistic, the goal is to find oneself in God. Tillich's claim that God, or Being-itself, is the Ground of our Being, our ultimate concern, proposes openly the ideal of self-coincidence as the highest value as well as the ultimate metaphysical reality. The person who wants to be his self, to be at one with himself, is asking that each act of consciousness, every choice and reaction, should issue unerringly from some source which he is absolutely. This would mean that his life would have absolute coherence and that each act would be "right" because it would be in perfect harmony with its self-center. This is the ideal of philosophies of self-realization from Aristotle to Erich Fromm. For Aristotle the ideal is supported by precisely the eternal Self-Cause which Sartre has rejected as a self-contradiction. In completely humanistic philosophies, self-realization is advocated at the price of human freedom. Once man is endowed with an innate essence which develops its potentialities like the acorn which becomes an oak tree, we can no longer call him a self-creating process.

Sartre says that self-coincidence or being God is the ideal of each one of us and that we all lead our lives as if the goal were attainable. Does this mean that each man's life is a self-deception? Or is the desire to be God a kind of original sin from which a brave few might rescue themselves? I should prefer, rather, to say that the goal of becoming Being-in-itself-for-itself is indeed inseparable from Being-for-itself, that it represents part of the paradox which human reality is. I believe that to describe man thus is to say something true about him. I think that to claim that he pursues an unattainable ideal is not to condemn him. Sartre does say that man is a useless passion. Useless in what way? Useless in that man's existence isn't *for* anything except himself. Useless in that his activity finds no ultimate support outside itself. Some will say that this is enough to condemn the human adventure, and it is true that Sartrean man does not find any final resting point inside or outside himself any more than Galileo could get to that outside vantage point from which he could use a lever to move the earth from its axis.

One may argue whether Sartre's description of consciousness does or does not fit our observations of human experience. To label it false because it seems to make man's existence meaningless and unhappy is poor philosophy. Furthermore, it is to assume arbitrarily that to live with a goal which cannot be completely achieved is in itself an evil. That man is characterized by negativity cannot be denied. Whether this is to condemn man to unhappiness is something else again. If Sartre had said that man is a creature of infinite aspiration, this would be the same as to argue that man is never finally at one with himself, but it would probably not evoke the pejorative connotations. Yet I do not want to take away the negative implications which Sartre intended to convey. For the human being to think that he can remain free and at the same time be guaranteed in this freedom, to think that he can live a perpetual self-creation and at the same time *be* a self, that he can at once be human and nonhuman, is error and self-deception. It is bad faith.

If we hold, however, that good faith means recognizing that freedom must be its own sole support, we do not necessarily give up the goal of self-coincidence *as a goal.* If I seek to live authentically, I try to harmonize my external actions with what I spontaneously feel to be a value worth preserving, a value which I have created as a value by choosing it. I acknowledge my authorship of past actions and the consequences which have resulted from them without denying that I am freely choosing now what I will do with them. I affirm the continuity of my psychic life without forgetting the Nothingness with which consciousness constantly enfolds it. I want to feel at every moment that the objectified self which my actions inscribe in the world is a true reflection of the free consciousness which willed it. I should like to think that at any later moment, my more experienced and more knowledgeable future self would reaffirm the honesty and wisdom of that choice, and that it would do so even after realizing its freedom to choose differently. This is to hope that there would be absolute equanimity between the Being-in-itself which I am, in the past, and my living for-itself. In its own way this is the desire to unite Being-in-itself and Being-for-itself. It is impossible to attain, but it is valid as an ideal.

One might compare the ideal of the In-itself-for-itself with that of absolute Truth. To assume that there is one final and ultimate Truth which includes the whole of things is naïve in the extreme. Even if we avoid the trap of thinking of Truth as an entity and view it as the ultimate harmony of reality and the propositions stated about reality—either by way of correspondence or pragmatically—Truth remains an ideal out of reach. To think that one has apprehended it in some final and absolute sense is to be furthest removed from it.

Yet, in the realm of knowledge, the closer we approximate to it, the greater our satisfaction.

As I live, I objectify myself. This past which I drag along behind me, this situation in which I found myself and which I have structured by an internalization—these belong to me; they are what makes me known to others, and I know myself through them. Yet I am always slightly beyond them, putting them into question. I can never wholly know myself, for I am not myself. I am perpetually making myself. My attempts to coincide with myself are doomed to failure. Still I am known somehow by others, and we have all but ignored this dimension of human existence until now. Is there any way to find rest in this game of self-pursuit by finding my Being in and with others? The relation between consciousnesses is another central theme in *Being and Nothingness*. Like the missing God, Sartre's view of human relations evoked a scandal of protests and has contributed more than any other factor to the conclusion that his philosophy could not produce a positive social theory. So strong was this conviction that when the social theory appeared, many critics concluded ahead of time that Sartre must have abandoned his early position, that he had simply exchanged existentialism for Marxism. Yet he himself has at no time renounced his earlier work. Conflict is stated to be the origin of human relations both in *Being and Nothingness* (1943) and in the *Critique* (1960).[2] And there is no mistaking Sartre's positive intentions in the later book. Obviously, in his own eyes at least, it is possible to move from conflict to solidarity.

[2] Original publication dates.

5

HELL IS OTHERS

If human relations are a failure, it is for one of two reasons: either they are in bad faith, or one demands of them something which they cannot give and which would be self-destructive if attained. Sartre discusses both of these causes in *Being and Nothingness*, but there is no denying that he leaves us with a major question unanswered. In introducing the subject of "Concrete Relations with Others," Sartre makes the preliminary statement that all human relations are variations on two primitive attitudes: (1) I attempt to absorb the Other's freedom while still maintaining it as freedom; I allow myself to be an object before it, but gladly in the hope that it will sustain me in my being, thus allowing me at long last to be coincident with myself. As manifestations of this attitude, Sartre considers love and masochism. (2) I try to possess the Other as an object so as to prevent him from ever threatening my own sovereign subjectivity. In this connection Sartre analyzes indifference, sadism, and hate.

Neither of these attempts can succeed. The first seeks to deny that I am a free subject and responsible for my being; the second more violently would do the same thing to another. Sartre seems to say as emphatically as anyone can that there is no other alternative. By way of introduction to his analysis of personal relations, he states:

There is no dialectic for my relations toward the Other but rather a circle—although each attempt is enriched by the failure of the other one. Thus we shall study each one in turn. But it should be noted that at the very core of each the other one remains always present, precisely because neither of the two can be held without contradiction. Better yet, each of them is in the other and endangers the death of the other. Thus we can never get outside of the circle. [p. 363]

At the end of his demonstration of the failure of each one of these attempts to relate to another person, Sartre concludes, "Nothing remains for the For-itself except to re-enter the circle and allow itself to be indefinitely tossed from one to the other of the two fundamental attitudes" (p. 412). It is hard to imagine statements much more definite and more negative than these. One can hardly blame readers for concluding that Sartre leaves no way out. It certainly appears that any hope of satisfactory human communication is as useless as the passion to be God, and we should be doing an injustice to Sartre if we tried to explain that somehow he did not really mean what he has said. Nevertheless, there is something important to be added. Immediately after the last quoted sentence, Sartre adds a surprising footnote: "These considerations do not exclude the possibility of an ethics of deliverance and salvation. But this can be achieved only after a radical conversion which we cannot discuss here." How are we to interpret this tantalizing, almost maddening, note? Is Sartre playing games with his reader? This is not the only place in *Being and Nothingness* in which he adds a closing footnote which suddenly seems to throw all the preceding material into question. At the end of his discussion of bad faith, Sartre suggests that it is indifferent whether we live in good or in bad faith, for "bad faith reapprehends good faith and slides to the very origin of the project of good faith." But he adds immediately that this does not mean that we can never escape bad faith—only that "this supposes a self-recovery of being which was previously corrupted. This self-recovery we shall call authenticity, the description of which has no place here." [p. 70] Elsewhere Sartre refers to a "purifying reflection" which he declines to explain. And, of course, the book ends with a promise of a volume on ethics, which would presumably have explained these positive aspects but which so far has remained as unrevealed as has the missing God.

We are left with an inevitable conclusion: Sartre considered that what he had described referred only to conduct in bad faith and believed that good faith and positive human relations are possible. Only a forlorn hope, say the hostile critics, and one which his ontology would not support. They have gone on to insist that whatever "radical conversion" Sartre may have had in mind when he wrote *Being and Nothingness*, the one which actually occurred in Sartre's life was his realization that subjective individualism could lead to no constructive social theory and that he consequently decided to commit his own freedom to Marxism. I doubt that we shall ever know exactly what sort of "conversion" Sartre originally had in mind, though it probably involved a philosophical attempt to envision an ethics based on the radical freedom of a consciousness which knows itself to be individual but not identical with any personality structure. The critics are right in one respect: Sartre's own conversion was political, and it led him to abandon the problem of individual ethics and to focus his attention directly on social and political theory.

It is significant that toward the end of the *Critique*, Sartre writes, "The group is defined and produces itself not only as an instrument but as a *mode of existence. . . .* [It] is both the most efficacious *means* of controlling the material environment in the compass of scarcity and the *absolute end* as a pure freedom liberating men from otherness." [1] In the group we are freed of our alien-ation, and it was the desire to recover ourselves which was the mainspring of the abortive attempts to establish a satisfying relation with the Other which Sartre had analyzed earlier. If we were to say that for Sartre the closest thing to salvation for contemporary man is to be found in the right kind of political commitment, we should not be altogether wrong. The statement is not very meaningful, however, and it is likely to be mis-leading unless we have traced the links between the isolated individual in *Being and Nothingness* and the member of the group-in-fusion in the *Critique*. This I hope to do later. At present we should turn our attention to the reasons for failure in personal human relations as they are commonly lived—in bad faith, according to Sartre, or at least mistakenly.

The nature of my relation with the Other and my first awakening to his existence are illustrated in Sartre's justly famous example of a person caught bending over a keyhole. Engrossed in his spying, he exemplifies the existential situation of each one of us as we nonreflec-tively live our conscious life. All is referred back to him as center of reference. He is all subject, for everything and everybody is an object of his consciousness. We have seen that my consciousness can never be an object to itself. Thus there is a qualitative difference between it and all that is outside it. Then as our spy hears foot-

[1] *Critique de la raison dialectique*, p. 639.

steps and straightens up to confront the judgmental stare of his witness, there is a dramatic reversal. Suddenly he perceives that he too has an object side. He *is* an object, but for another consciousness, not for himself. Sartre has been criticized for basing his revelation of the Other on the hostile stare or indifferent look rather than on a moment of meaningful communication. But what matters is not the emotional overtones of his examples, but the question of whether or not he is correct in seeing all human relations in terms of subjects and objects.

Sartre's discussion of Being-for-others is a natural extension of his analysis of one's attempt to be oneself. We have observed the way in which the For-itself, in reflection, tries to *be* the self which it pursues; that is, to be simultaneously Being-in-itself and Being-for-itself or to be both subject and object to itself. In my relations with others I try once more to succeed in this effort at self-recovery. The goal is to be simultaneously myself and other. As Plato put it, love is the desire and pursuit of the whole. Unity with the Other, a unity in which two free subjects become a single transcendence, is "the ideal of love, its motivation and its end, its unique value" (*Being and Nothingness*, p. 366). Sartre declares this ideal to be unattainable both factually and theoretically. If the voices of countless poets and mystics rise up to declare him wrong, we must consider whether they do not in fact speak in metaphor only and whether, in any case, the unity which they declare is not something other than that of subject consciousnesses. To be united as subject with another subject would mean to "exist his body" (Sartre's expression) in the same way as he exists it and as I exist my own but without ceasing to "exist my own." It would be to know the taste of his mouth as he tastes it. It would mean not only to comprehend from within his whole psychic structure but to be one with the movement by which his consciousness reflects on it. Most important of all, it would mean that I would erase all separation between us without depriving him of his quality of otherness. I would have to become him without ceasing to be myself. We are not speaking here of a sharing but of a being.

It seems to me obvious that Sartre is correct in declaring the ideal unattainable. Someone might object that clearly nobody who speaks of the union of lovers means it so literally, and I agree. But if we were to press the question, I doubt that we should find much unanimity as to exactly what kind of unity is left when metaphor has been stripped away. I suspect we would discover not that there has been a union of consciousnesses but rather a mutual agreement not to exploit the object side of either member of the couple in such a way as to injure him as subject. This is entirely permissible in Sartrean terms, but it is a far cry from the attainment of the original goal of love. Sartre insists that the presence of this ideal is always hovering in the background of the enterprise of love, that its impossibility accounts for the *amari aliquid*, the bitter tinge of frustration in even the most passionate of love affairs, and that the pretense that the ideal is attainable is the origin of those personal relations which are exploitative and in bad faith whether they pass for love or openly as hate.

Sartre's analysis of love (*l'amour*) is of erotic love or of the state we call "being in love." It might by extension apply to certain forms of parental love or of any love which is primarily a means of personal fulfillment. It is not to be identified with compassion or a sense of human solidarity. Within this limited context,

Sartre declares that love is the desire to be loved. In love, I want to act on the Other's freedom but still want to maintain it as freedom. I value and respect his subjectivity; in one respect I even place it above my own, for what I desire from him is that he should found my being. Yet this does not mean that I want to be an object for him in the way that I am an object for anybody else. I do not wish simply that I should be an object *for him* but that through his intermediacy he might constitute me as an object for myself. In short, I want him to serve as the foundation of my being by objectifying the subjective world which I have established. If I can so act on his freedom that he will freely support and make my world the center of his, then it seems that I—through identifying my freedom with his—have become my own foundation. I need no longer fear the Other's look, for he consents to look as with my eyes; yet since he is outside my consciousness, he gives to my being the objectivity which it could never find by itself. It is my free subjectivity which I want to be loved, not what I have done. This is the origin of the pathetic desire for those promises that one will be loved forever no matter what he may do or become. I seek a pledge to ensure that I, a free existence, am endowed with an absolutely valued essence, that I am myself.

Aside from the ontological contradictions in such a demand, Sartre asserts that there are three pitfalls which bring about the failure of love. First, if my love is returned, if the Other consents to found my being by securing it as the center of his concern, his love demands being loved in turn by me. Therefore, I am thrown back on my own being once again. I cannot avoid the responsibility of pursuing my self rather than being it. Second, the Other may always revoke his consent.

I may suddenly find that instead of being an encapsulated subject-as-object, I am purely an object. Finally, even granted that one Other and I succeed for a brief moment in asserting the absolute being of one another's private worlds, we are not invulnerable to the Look of a third person who may suddenly transform us both into alienated objects. Love as an escape from my own subjectivity is a blind alley.

That many people try to make of love only a self-fulfillment is undeniable. Personally, I think Sartre is right in denying that in love there is any escape from that ultimate isolation which is the inextricable accompaniment of being a free consciousness, a For-itself individualized by its attachment to the particular part of Being which we call the human body. It is easy to see why Sartre feels that a love which seeks to escape from the burden of lonely responsibility slips so easily into masochism. If in despair I give up the ideal of finding objective support for my Being-as-subject, I may will to surrender that freedom—more precisely, to escape from it by becoming only an object. If in humiliation and pain I feel myself to be used as a thing by someone who does not love me, the very fact that I suffer seems to testify that I am what I am without having chosen it. Sartre goes on to explain that this attitude, too, carries the seed of its own failure. In order to grasp myself once and for all as object, I would have to see myself as the Other sees me. But it is only for him that I am obscene or disgusting or ridiculous. The more my objectness satisfies me, the more its negative qualities escape me. "The more [the masochist] tries to taste his objectivity, the more he will be submerged by the consciousness of his subjectivity—hence his anguish" (p. 378).

Since I cannot grasp the self which I am for others and thereby be it for myself, since I cannot control the quality of the object-self which the Other sees, my recourse is to tumble over into the second of the two original attitudes toward others. I try to make of the Other only an object so that at least my own subjectivity may be invulnerable, so that he can never make me in turn the object of any look. Clearly such an attitude is in bad faith, for it is based on the premise that the Other is not a subject or that he can be stripped of his subjectivity. In any case it fails to reach its goal.

I may start by adopting an attitude of indifference toward all others, moving among them as if they were in truth only things in the world. I may see in a waiter or a clerk, an employee or a student, nothing but his function. I may try to manipulate people as if they were robots by learning "what makes them tick." This procedure is not only futile but dangerous. At any moment one of these machines may suddenly direct on me an altogether human look, and the game is up. The "indifferent" man must realize that he moves as if amid a collection of high explosives.

As love may lead to masochism, so one may fall from sexual desire into sadism. Although Sartre says that desire is an attempt to get hold of the Other's subjectivity by making him into an object, his discussion of eroticism suggests more mutuality and even generosity than does his analysis of love. He holds that the caress is the language of desire. It is "an appropriation of the Other's body," and it represents, for Sartre, a more fundamental expression of sexuality than even the tumescence of the genital organs. Admitting that the possession of a particular sex—both the specific sexual organs and the secondary sexual characteristics—is purely fortuitous and contingent, Sartre argues that sexuality is not "a contingent accident bound to our physiological nature"; its explanation is not on the level of biology. Rather, it is "a necessary structure of being-for-itself-for-others," and its description belongs with ontology.

Man, it is said, is a sexual being because he possesses a sex. And if the reverse were true? If sex were only the instrument and, so to speak, the image of a fundamental sexuality? If man possessed a sex only because he is originally and fundamentally a sexual being as a being who exists in the world in relation with other men? . . . There is one mode of sexuality "with the possibility of satisfaction," and the developed sex represents and makes concrete this possibility. But there are other modes of sexuality of the type which cannot get satisfaction, and if we take these modes into account we are forced to recognize that sexuality appears with birth and disappears only with death. [pp. 383–84]

Sartre makes sexuality as basic to human existence as does Freud; all human relations are sexual to some degree. But there is one tremendous difference. For Freud, movement of the libido is determined from the start by the biological characteristics inherent in a particular sex, and these influence the total personality structure. Woman is a *sexe manqué*. Her "feminine character" is conditioned by biology even more than by social custom. Freud seems to imply that one is a man or a woman before one is human, that the direction of one's purely human development is determined at birth. It is this idea which Simone de Beauvoir has so effectively attacked in *The Second Sex*, and the philosophical premise which supports her "feminist" position is derived from Sartrean ontology. Obviously, the sexual life of a For-itself will be significantly different according to its "accidental" sexual differentiation, but this is only the starting point. As with any other aspect of one's facticity (one's body, the time and place of one's birth), there is an infinity of possible ways in which one may weave one's sexuality into the warp and woof of one's life.

Sexual desire, for Sartre, is a desire for a body, a wish to possess the Other as flesh, but it is certainly not the desire to possess a body as a thing, as nothing but In-itself. It is the desire for a particular body "with consciousness on the horizon." More specifically, it is the desire to ensnare consciousness in the body so that what one possesses is no longer simply body but embodied consciousness.

The caress is an appropriation of the Other's body. It is evident that if caresses were only a stroking or brushing of the surface, there could be no relation between them and the powerful desire which they claim to fulfill; they would remain on the surface like looks and could not *appropriate* the Other for me. . . . The caress is the ensemble of those rituals which incarnate the Other. [pp. 389–90]

Desire aims at incarnating the Other, but it can be fulfilled only by the simultaneous incarnation of oneself. The lover, by his caresses, induces the beloved to become willingly a passive flesh beneath his fingers, but this flesh can be enjoyed only if the lover freely consents to his own incarnation. Thus physical possession is a "reciprocal incarnation" whether one views oneself as possessing or possessed. To the extent that each one has made himself a flesh-consciousness, there has been reciprocity, but this is not the same as a union of consciousnesses. Desire is doomed to failure by the very fact that it is fulfilled as desire. The desire to possess or to be possessed by another as Other becomes converted into the desire for pleasure. The reciprocal incarnation is broken.

Sartre claims that sadism stems from the half-realized recognition that desire has somehow failed to attain its original object. The sadist wants to reduce the Other to facticity, to make the Other only a flesh-consciousness without incarnating himself. Thus the sadist, whether sexually or otherwise, openly uses the Other as an instrument. His aim is achieved at that point when the Other's consciousness finally yields to the tortured body's demands, abnegating its commitment to the values which it had cherished. At that point the sadist tastes the joy of being total subject in command of a captive freedom—or so he hopes, but Sartre points out that sadism, too, ends in failure. The sadist can never possess the Other's freedom as freedom. To the degree that he has succeeded in making the Other into an object, he may feel that he possesses that object; he does not possess a subject. More important, the free subjectivity of the victim has never been fully overcome. It is he who determines the exact time and manner of his abjuration and the way in which he will live the memory of it. Moreover, at the moment of the sadist's greatest triumph, the victim may look at his torturer. And at that instant all the sadist's efforts are seen to have been in vain.

At this point the only recourse is hate. Sartre describes hate as a wish for the death of the Other, a wish which is explained by the fact that I want to wipe out forever the self which I have been for another. For the Other's look is not erased by time. Once it has appeared, it endures forever. If I feel that I have been a ridiculous or evil or cowardly object in another's consciousness, I may wish that I could wipe out that consciousness completely. Sartre points out that hatred of a particular Other is in reality hatred of all others. If I wish to erase the self-for-others which I have been, if I do not wish to be my self-for-others, logically I should have to destroy all others. But hate too is futile. Even if all others ceased to be, the memory of the Other's look would live on forever in my own conscious memory, inseparable from whatever idea I might try to form of my object self. The exaggerated fear of the power of the Other to transform me into a thing, to make me only that object which I must be for him and not myself, gives rise to what Sartre calls the Medusa complex, referring to the Greek Gorgon who by her look turned people into stone. The eye of God is related to this same idea, not only God as the eternal and omnipresent subject before whom I am forever a helpless object but the God who by his all-powerful regard might be induced to bestow on me the objectified self-for-others which I would like to be. Just as God is the self-coincidence toward which I vainly aspire in my pursuit of self, so he is also the ideal Other in whom I might find my being without losing my freedom. Neither God exists. I can neither be myself nor lose myself.

I think anyone would admit that many, if not most, human relations display the ingredients of the subject-object conflict. The important question is whether the patterns Sartre has described are to be considered as examples of relations in bad faith or whether all human relations are based on conflict and doomed to failure. I think that we cannot arrive at a really satisfactory answer until we have considered Sartre's discussion of the group in the *Critique*. But there are a few observations which may be made even at this early stage.

First, as I have attempted to show elsewhere,[2] there are two aspects of the Look which allow, if they do not imply, much more positive possibilities than those which we have considered. Although *le regard* is neutral in its implications, most of Sartre's examples and terminology seem to justify interpreting it as the stare of judgment or of hostility. It is that which comes to me unexpectedly and suddenly transforms me from subject to object, even though sometimes—as in pride—I feel that I am the object of admiration. But the Look is not always unexpected, and it can be deliberately sought. The Look may also be an exchange. And two people may look at the world together. Looking-at-the-world-together (not of two only but of a group) is a major theme in the *Critique*, where Sartre describes the emergence of a "We" which finds its unity out there in the world by dint of our common project. The Look-as-exchange belongs still in the realm of private relations. This is not a union of subjects but a mutual affirmation of respect for the Other as subject. It resembles Sartre's enterprise of love but lacks the attempt to assimilate the Other's freedom. Sartre has never analyzed this possibility in philosophical terms, but we can find examples of it in his fiction. Finally, we may say of human communication what we observed with regard to the project of trying to become God. The fact that a goal is unattainable does not mean that it cannot have what Santayana describes as the drawing power of the higher ideal, even

[2] I have discussed this material in much more detail in my book *An Existentialist Ethics* (New York: Alfred A. Knopf, 1967).

when, as in this case, the attainment of the ideal would
be its self-destruction.

We have seen that, for Sartre, freedom and responsibility are inseparable. Freedom "creates the objects from which we suffer," as we saw in *Bariona*. It
"enchains itself in the world as a free project toward
ends" (*Being and Nothingness*, p. 551). But freedom
is not gratuitous. We "use our own scales" to weigh each
act and every final end (pp. 470–71). Freedom has two
limits: I am not free not to be free, and thus freedom
is limited by itself; and I am limited by the freedom of
the Other, who can always bestow on my life and my
projects an outside which I have not chosen. We have
observed how Sartre's claims for freedom derive directly
from his concept of consciousness. We can understand
how this two-edged freedom appears in a different light
depending on one's situation and one's own choice of
being. To Roquentin, who sought an escape from the
meaningless contingency of the world, freedom was revealed in nausea. To Orestes, who looked for some kind
of moral authority outside himself, freedom was revealed
first in despair but was transformed into deliverance
when Orestes engaged himself in a course of action to
which he himself assigned its value. To Bariona, who
was already committed to the cause of political freedom, the revelation was in literal truth a "joy to the
world." If Mathieu, in Sartre's novel *The Age of Reason*,
found that he was free for nothing, it was because he
had chosen noninvolvement.

Before we approach the problem of Sartre's grow-
ing commitment to political action, we should consider
at least briefly the relation between his philosophy and
his imaginative literature. Three plays—*No Exit, Dirty*

Hands, and *The Condemned of Altona*—seem to me particularly relevant and significant for our purpose. In looking at these examples, I think we shall find that the treatment of time is an important dimension of the literature as well as of the philosophy. We shall observe in concrete situations some of the consequences of Sartre's view of individual psychology and personal relations. Finally, we shall see, both in the dramas themselves and in comments which Sartre has made concerning them, the first steps toward that radical conversion which seems at present to have led Sartre to abandon literature.

6

PHILOSOPHY IN LITERATURE

回 回 回

In his autobiography Sartre remarks that he began his life as he will doubtless end it—among books. Before he had learned to read for himself, he insisted on having his own books; he "looked upon teaching as a priesthood and literature as a passion." Even the adult Sartre, by his own admission, reads a good detective story "with more pleasure than Wittgenstein."[1] As a boy he disappointed his grandfather by devoting himself, with an enthusiasm bordering on frenzy, to cheap adventure stories, and he even wrote some of his own. We can see traces of this fascination in Roquentin's desire to transform his life into literature. Sartre has said of himself that it took him fifty years to awake from the dream of attaining salvation through writing. We must note, however, that the period definitely includes two stages. In *Nausea* we can still see traces of the child Sartre's desire to become one of the immortals through literature, to find his true life posthumously. By the time of *Bariona* we find him already using literature as a form of political action. Immediately after the war, Sartre was foremost in proclaiming the doctrine of engaged literature, which he presented in the first issue of *Les Temps modernes* and developed in *What Is Literature?*

If Sartre during these years still regarded the writer as somehow privileged, he explicitly renounced both the ideal of "art for art's sake" and any notion that a legiti-

[1] *Les Mots*, p. 61.

mate goal for the writer was the esteem of future generations. "We write for our own time," he declared in an article under that title, and not for posterity. Sartre was criticized for confusing engaged literature with simple propaganda, and he himself felt it necessary to point out that the artist owes an allegiance to his art as well as an obligation to society. But while he insisted that the writer must be free as a writer, Sartre argued that literature, which derives from man's freedom, must always be addressed to the cause of human freedom. Already he was wrestling with the problem of how the writer could address himself directly to the masses he wanted to liberate. The question is one for which Sartre has not personally found any satisfactory answer. He is as well aware as anyone else that his *Critique de la raison dialectique* is not much more likely to be read by the average French factory worker than by a Hindu peasant. There is, however, an excellent chance that a significant number of workers will see a play by Sartre or a film based on the play. Even though the last part of his career has seen Sartre neglecting literature for politics—reminiscent of Plato's pained decision to banish the poets from the Republic—the opportunity to influence society was one of Sartre's earlier justifications for giving to literature a privileged position and to the creative writer a special trust.

We may say that Sartre's choice of a career divided between philosophy and literature is explained partly by his personal biography and partly by his desire to employ drama and other forms of fiction as an effective means of putting his ideas within the grasp of a wider audience than one solely of philosophers and scholars. There is a third factor at least as important as the other two. If we find it difficult to imagine Descartes or Kant as writers of fiction, this is not entirely because of their particular temperaments or the uncongeniality of their style. At least in Sartre's view, imagination is as necessary for philosophers as for other creative thinkers. But it would be hard to see how either the Cartesian or the Kantian concept of reality would benefit by being clothed with the flesh and blood of fictional characters and worked out in the context of the everyday world. Existentialism since its beginning has tended to bridge the gap between the theoretical and the literary. Kierkegaard's pseudonyms, his anecdotal "Diary of a Seducer" in *Either/Or* and "Symposium" in *Stages on Life's Way* have at least presented imaginary characters. Marcel has written plays. Camus, while not strictly a philosopher or formally an existentialist, certainly has presented, in both fiction and philosophical essays, ideas associated with existentialism. And of course there is Simone de Beauvoir, whose novels and one play work with themes either derived from Sartre's philosophy or discussed in essays of her own.

This development has come about naturally for a number of reasons. Kierkegaard's existentialism started as an attempt to reaffirm against Hegel the irreducible significance of the living individual, the impossibility of absorbing him into any system, the irreconcilability of opposites, the subjectivity of all apprehended truth. Kierkegaard was concerned with existential anguish and despair as they are felt in concrete situations and with the uniqueness of any lived situation. All of this cried out for the necessity of presenting not one totalizing view of reality, but many partial experiences of the real. What better suited for this purpose than imaginative literature?

For Sartre, too, literature offers the opportunity to

explore the possibilities of watching human beings make themselves, choose their being in the process of relating themselves to the outside world. But there is still another reason for him to have found in literature a natural outlet for what he wished to say. This is found in his theory of imagination as he developed it in *L'Imaginaire* (*The Psychology of Imagination*).

Sartre argues that imagination (like perception or emotion) is a mode of consciousness and an essential structure of consciousness. His theory is in sharp contrast with traditional psychology, which attempted to explain the image by relating it to the perception. Sartre argues that perceiving and imagining represent two totally distinct mental functions. Perception, as we have seen, involves a nihilating act of consciousness, one which posits an object by means of "wrapping it in a shell of nothingness." But no matter how consciousness may perceive its object, clearly or inaccurately, as a focal center or as a background field, perception is always and solely concerned with the real. Even memory is addressed to the real, and so is the anticipation of the immediate future of my action—for example, when I move my eyes toward the area of the tennis court where I expect my opponent's ball to fall. Sartre compares memory and anticipation with the way in which my eye and mind complete the design of the arabesque of a carpet which is partially covered by a table leg.

In all these instances, one is attempting to fill out a form, part of which is clearly given, the rest taken as equally real though not fully revealed. In every case the real is the measure of the perception. Most important of all, my original perception can be enriched by a return to the original object. For Sartre, as for Husserl and all succeeding phenomenologists, the object reveals itself to my perceiving in an inexhaustible series of profiles or *Abschattungen* (shadings) correlated with my eye movements. If I look at a building, I see the precise number of the columns on the face confronting me. If I look away and forget how many there are, another act of perception will enable me to count them. In contrast, the image is given all at once; once I have formed it, there is no way in which my consciousness may return to it for further enrichment or corroboration. I may produce a series of images of buildings with varying numbers of columns *ad infinitum*, but the image itself will never teach me anything.

Imagination introduces the unreal. An image as such, of course, is a real object of consciousness; that is, I can always reflectively consider my own imaginings. But if I have an image of a dead or absent friend, it is the friend who is the object of my consciousness, but my friend as imagined, not as perceived. The act of imagining involves a double nihilation. First, I nihilate the world as a totality by psychically withdrawing from it (that is, the whole of things is constituted as a world by my nihilating consciousness); then I constitute the image as not belonging to it. For example, if I form an image of Pierre, who is dead, I first constitute the world as a totality from which he is absent, then constitute an image of Pierre as nonexisting.

It should be obvious that this analysis of imagination is not very different from Sartre's description of the activity of a free consciousness as such. Sartre himself stresses this fact. Without the possibility of imagining —i.e., creating the unreal—man would be wholly engulfed, swallowed up in the real.

This conception of a consciousness mired in the world is not unknown to us, for it is precisely that of psychological determinism. We can boldly assert that if consciousness is a succession of determined psychic facts, it is totally impossible for it to produce anything other than the real. In order for a consciousness to be able to imagine, it must escape from the world by its very nature, it must be able to effect from itself a withdrawal in relation to the world. In a word, it must be free.[2]

In imagination, even though the objects of my images may exist in the world, I deal with them as unreal; hence I control them. In *The Psychology of Imagination*, Sartre describes vividly how lovers may indulge in imaginings of the absent beloved until they come to love the image rather than the reality. If "absence makes the heart grow fonder" and if reunions are at first somewhat disillusioning, this is because my memories and anticipations have not been wholly directed toward the real but concerned with setting up unreal images in which the Other acts not out of his own freedom but in conformance with my own needs and expectations. Encounter with the real person is far more enriching than my impoverished images—and more disturbing. Sartre has no patience with those who prefer living in imagined pasts and futures rather than in real ones. The case is different for imaginative literature, though obviously Sartre would disapprove of a Madame Bovary who attempts to construct life after the pattern of the novels she borrows from the lending library. In Emma's case, both she and the authors she reads are at fault. For through their imagined world, they falsify the real world.

At the end of *What Is Literature?* Sartre speaks of literature in almost the same terms in which he spoke of imagination. If literature were to become pure prop-

[2] *L'Imaginaire* (Paris: Gallimard, 1940), pp. 233–34.

aganda or pure entertainment, he says, we would be "glued to" the real; "society would wallow in the immediate, that is, in the life without memory of hymenoptera and gasteropods." [3] He concludes that while the universe could certainly get along without literature, it could do without man even better. Sartre maintains that the aesthetic object, both in creation and in enjoyment, is unreal. The artist in creation and the viewer, reader, or listener in a "guided creation" must evoke this unreal object on each occasion that it exists. He points out that in a painting of Charles VIII, the object of perception is canvas, pigments, wooden frame, brush strokes, and so forth. "Charles VIII" is an image which I must sustain by canceling out the materials which compose it. Even more clearly, the black-and-white printed words of a novel are not the aesthetic object. In order to evoke the characters and the story, to make them real as images, I must nihilate both the material book and my own materiality in my particular situation.

In reading a work of fiction, or in absorbed watching of a play or film, I experience imaginatively a oneness of consciousnesses which has no counterpart in the real world. I am inside the private world of the Other. So far we might say that literature represents purely imaginary wish-fulfillment, and this is perhaps true for people who read uncritically only that literature which reflects back to them their own picture of what they would like to see reality as being. But Sartre makes a further point. Even in the imaginary mode, the object aimed at is ultimately the real world. The object of the image of my friend

[3] This work was published in *Situations II* (Paris: Gallimard, 1948) as "Qu'est-ce que la Littérature?" I have quoted from the English translation by Bernard Frechtman, *What Is Literature?* (New York: Philosophical Library, 1949).

is the real friend whether he still lives or not. I may, to be sure, imagine a centaur or a Martian and know that it is unreal. Even this is to affirm that the real world is such that these existents are definitely excluded. In fantasy as in "realistic" literature, whether negatively or positively, a definite attitude toward the real world is postulated and the real world is affected.

There is a sense in which even the fictitious character returns my look. If I enter the imaginary world of the fictional being, I thereby introduce him into my own world, and its structures are modified by his presence. Engaged literature seeks to fulfill more deliberately the function of any literature. It puts the familiar real into question by holding up an imaginary world for us to contemplate. The writer who seeks to enlist our sympathies for the oppressed compels us not merely to know but to feel what it is like to be this kind of victim in this sort of situation.

There is a less obvious and more specifically existentialist way in which literature may serve to illuminate the human situation. This is best illustrated by our reactions when we read appreciatively a book which does not urge on us a cause to which we are already committed or which easily enlists our sympathy. Suppose, for example, I read Jean Genet's *Our Lady of the Flowers* without having been exposed to Sartre's sympathetic biography of Genet. Unless I belong to a small minority of readers, I do not approve of robbery, homosexual prostitution, or personal treachery against a friend; neither do I make heroes out of condemned murderers—even if I don't like capital punishment. Furthermore, Genet strictly forbids me to see his characters as pathetic victims of society who could be reformed by a bit of psychiatric counseling and the offer of a steady job.

Assuming that Genet seduces me into finishing his book, I read it with a perpetual ambivalence that is profoundly disturbing. My approval is not won or even sought, yet my sympathies are engaged. I read the underside of my conventional judgments and find there a despair and an exultation, a corruption and a heroism which I have been forced to experience briefly as perhaps valid, certainly not to be wiped out. Paradoxically, my imaginative sharing of another's life results in my reflective realization of the distance between the private worlds of isolated living subjects. I lose my illusory belief in the absolute, impersonal reality of what we like to think is the objective world. I discover that the world bears a multiplicity of countenances which can never be resolved into one. The social context is no longer a solid entity but rather a scaffolding permeated with empty spaces, each providing for a new point of view on the total structure.

The writing of fiction offered Sartre not only the fulfillment of aspirations formed before he was ten years old but the opportunity to influence society by changing people's attitudes toward it and their way of thinking about themselves. As one might have expected, he very early announced his intention to break with the traditional literature of characters and to deal rather with a literature of situations. This resolution was in perfect conformity with his own philosophy as well as with his concern for political action. The psychological studies of character which had dominated the novel even before Freud were based on the notion of a character's developing slowly and inevitably as the result of the influences of heredity and environment. Sartre preferred to show his readers and theater audiences human beings who chose themselves by choosing between opposing passions in moments of crisis. The choice is at once existential, moral, and political. If we see ourselves in these characters, it is not because we have certain psychological traits in common with them but because their situation and their choices represent for us real possibilities.

No Exit

Huis-clos (1944; *No Exit,* 1946) lacks entirely any overt political implications or call to action of the kind we observed in *Bariona.* At first thought one might question whether it is properly to be classified as engaged literature. On the other hand, it is more obviously linked with philosophical ideas proposed in *Being and Nothingness* than any other play of Sartre's except possibly *The Flies.* It has proved to be one of the most popular of his plays and the most frequently performed as well, certainly an indication that *No Exit* is more than a dramatized philosophical demonstration.

Hell is both literally and metaphorically the dramatic setting for *No Exit.* Hell is literally a great hotel where people are sent for punishment after death. The three characters who occupy one room of it are cut off completely from their individual situations on earth. They cannot go back. Metaphorically, Hell is real life as most people live it. Garcin's line "Hell is others" means both that the administrators of Hell have economically chosen to use the victims themselves to torment one another and that human relations anywhere are Hell. There are two time schemes. Within the room is eternity. On several occasions one of the characters is able to see events, invisible to the others or to the audience, which take place back on earth. These reported scenes give indication of the passing of time, change of seasons, and the like. They bear no relation whatsoever to the time of the stage action. In truth, there is no time in Hell, not only because Sartre is using the old notion that time is everywhere equidistant from eternity, but because existence after death lacks the essential characteristic which time possesses for Sartre. Time for a living consciousness is a process of remaking the past and choosing a future. Because of time the For-itself continually puts the meaning of its life into question and decides anew what it is. In *No Exit* the action moves in a circle. Garcin's closing words, "Let's get on with it. . . . ," indicate that everything is about to continue as before. Nobody will change, for this is Hell. Sartre says of death that it is the point at which the For-itself becomes In-itself. Others, not I, are responsible for my life. The dead are "the prey of the living." As each member of the triad is allowed a glimpse of what is happening in his former place on earth, he watches the living decide what has been the meaning of the dead person's life. Once this is fixed, he has no more visions. The experience for Inez is the most horrible of all. There is nobody among those who knew her who any longer thinks of her. New inhabitants of her room are aware of its having had a former occupant; but soon they make the room their own, and she is forgotten, one of the nameless dead. The fact that the three characters in the play are dead closes the door to any hope that they might change their behavior. The situation is like that in Dante's Hell. As they chose themselves in life, so they are fixed in eternity.

If we consider the characters not as dead but as living there before us, they display various attitudes in bad faith and the subject-object conflict or "battle to the death of consciousnesses" which Sartre analyzes in *Being and Nothingness*. The Look is naked hostility. We see its manifestations both in the interaction of the trio and in the confessions they make of their previous conduct. Indeed, their attitudes toward one another are but a continuation of their habitual patterns of human relations. Inez seems at least to avoid inauthenticity inasmuch as she does not try to deceive herself or others, but this does not mean that she is in good faith. She tells her companions that she is rotten to the core, but her attitude suggests that this is her given nature, that she could not be otherwise. She illustrates pure sadism. Describing a lesbian relationship, Inez makes it clear that she had not only treated Florence brutally but had used her as an instrument to torture Florence's husband. Specifically, she had compelled Florence to see the man as Inez saw him, and between them they drove him to his death. The failure of sadism is neatly demonstrated by the fact that one night Florence, the object victim, turned subject and asphyxiated both Inez and herself. On stage Inez tries to set up the same sort of relationship with Estelle. Unsuccessful because of the presence of Garcin, to whom Estelle feels much more attracted, she gives vent to her sadistic impulses by taking on the role of the Look of the Third.

Garcin makes a show of being as truthful as Inez by confessing to comparable conduct toward his wife. In this wretched woman, who willingly sought to be made wholly an object, we see masochism counterpoised to, and intertwined with, Garcin's and Inez's sadism. But Garcin's seemingly open confession is a disguise for what really bothers him—the fact that when his political convictions were tested, he had run away. We see him trying to remake his past but in bad faith, by pretending that his intentions should not be measured by what he had done. It is at this point that Inez tells him, "You *are* your life." Still, even though the fact is that he was on a train headed for the border when he was arrested, the past, because it is past, seems to allow for reinterpretation if an Other will support it. Garcin approaches Estelle. He and she now attempt by means of the erotic to establish what Sartre had declared to be the goal of love; that is, each one will serve as a subject to support the other as the object she or he would like to be. Estelle will shelter Garcin from the Look which would make him a coward; Garcin will return to Estelle her image of herself as pure and innocent, like "a glancing stream." They fail, of course, and for two reasons. First, Estelle is willing to accept Garcin simply as a man and is apparently truthful in telling him that she does not care at the moment whether he was a coward or not. She has neither the sensitivity to see nor the will to satisfy his desire to be reassured of the fact that she does not believe him to have been a coward. Second, just when it seems that they might succeed in bolstering one another's self-images, Inez is there to jeer at Garcin the deserter and Estelle the child murderer. Garcin abandons Estelle and proceeds to try to convince Inez that his acts had not been those of a coward, but we know that the Look of Estelle—if not Inez herself—will thwart him. The circular movement continues. Even when the door suddenly opens, no one of the three will leave. There is no exit, for each feels that he must protect himself against the Look which the other two might use to make him an object. There is no escape from the Other, for the Look is not tied to a pair of eyes which are physically present.

"Hell is others," says Garcin. Within the play itself, Hell is apparently the conflict of subjectivities, and this interpretation is certainly consistent with the ideas Sartre had expressed in *Being and Nothingness*. The room itself seems incidental, though the point is made that the authorities have left nothing to chance—that the color and position of the sofas, for instance, have been planned, the implication being that the setting would lend itself subtly to promoting the inevitable conflict. Philosophically the physical setting appears to have little meaning. Perhaps it underscores the point that the For-itself always exists in a definite situation in space and time (here the furnishings are of the period of the Second Empire). In the light of Sartre's *Critique*, one could retrospectively apply the term "worked-over matter" to the room and its furniture, for the three persons certainly enter into a room prepared for them by others. But the emphasis on the subjective aspect of human relations makes it seem hardly worthwhile to attempt to find specific significance in the environment—or so it seemed in the 1940s.

In 1964 Sartre granted an interview to *Playboy* during which he was asked to explain what he had meant by Garcin's "Hell is others." His reply was surprising.

Other people are hell insofar as you are plunged from birth into a situation to which you are obliged to submit. You are born the son of a rich man, or an Algerian, or a doctor, or an American. Then you have a cut-and-dried future mapped out, a future made for you by others. They haven't created it directly, but they are part of a social order that makes you what you are. If you're a peasant's son, the social order obliges you to move to the city where machines await you, machines that need fellows like you to keep them going. So it's your fate to be a certain type of worker, a country kid who has been driven away from the country by a certain type of capitalist pressure. Now the factory is a function of your being. What exactly *is* your "being"? It is the job you're doing, a job that masters you completely because it wears you down—along with your pay, which classifies you exactly by your standard of living. All this has been thrust on you by other people. Hell is the proper description for that kind of existence. Or take a child who was born in Algeria in 1930 or 1935. He was doomed to an explosion into death and the tortures that were his destiny. That, too, is hell.[4]

Sartre went on to say, "You can take action against what people have made of you and transform yourself." His response is not to be taken as advocating pure determinism. All the same, I am convinced that while *No Exit* may have meant to Sartre in 1964 what he said of it then, we have in this interview an impressive example of Sartre's point that we are free to remake our past. I believe that the determining influence of the social environment was not uppermost in his mind when he wrote the play. The shift in emphasis which took place over twenty years does not, however, represent an illogical or inconsistent development. It is, rather, a movement from the Look of the individual to the Look of the collectivity.

Dirty Hands

In *Les Mains sales* (1948; *Dirty Hands*, 1949), the action is centered on the efforts of an individual to come to grips with his past, but we are no longer dealing with a simple matter of bad faith. Reduced to essentials, the

[4] "Playboy Interview: Jean-Paul Sartre," *Playboy*, May, 1965, pp. 69–76.

plot, inspired by the murder of Trotsky, is as follows: Hugo, a young intellectual who has joined the Proletarian Party in Illyria, has agreed to carry out orders to kill Hoederer, a party leader who is planning political action which is not in keeping with the party line. In the role of secretary, he has come with his wife to live at Hoederer's home. Admiration for Hoederer and a dawning conviction that possibly he is in the right after all cause Hugo to delay. Finally, after another party member has already thrown a bomb into the villa, Hugo draws a revolver on Hoederer but is persuaded by him to drop it. Hoederer invites Hugo to work with him, and Hugo goes out in the garden to think the matter over. Returning to announce that he has decided affirmatively, he finds Hoederer with Hugo's wife in his arms. Hugo shoots him.

Sartre had originally thought of calling the play "Crime Passionel," which is the title of the translation published in England. It carries an appropriate ambiguity. Hugo's act was certainly a crime of passion. It was performed nonreflectively at a moment of extreme emotion. But was the passion personal or political? Several years later, after he has served a prison sentence, Hugo is asked this question by party members, and he himself does not know the answer. Yet everything depends on his reply. Hugo finds that the party line has altered; Hoederer had but anticipated the change and is now a hero. If Hugo says that the assassination was for political reasons, the party would find it highly inconvenient to have him still around. If he is willing to state that he shot Hoederer solely out of jealousy, he will be allowed to change his name and work for the party again.

The play opens with a short scene in which Hugo is asked by Olga, a former comrade, why he killed Hoederer. It closes with another, equally brief, in which he learns why the question is important and gives his answer. Within this framework are presented the events leading up to the assassination and the actual murder. This use of the flashback technique is certainly not significant in itself. If it offers anything unusual, it is only the fact that there is a slight ambiguity about the relation between the action we see on the stage and the account which Hugo gave Olga. That they are not identical is indicated by the fact that Olga later asks questions which she would not have asked if she had witnessed what the audience has seen. Apparently we are shown by the author what is supposed to have actually happened and are left in ignorance of what Hugo told Olga. There is no suggestion of Hugo's having falsified the past deliberately or through inaccurate memory. The problem lies in establishing what his motives were when he shot Hoederer, not what events really occurred. I suspect that Sartre has intended us to see the action directly so that we will realize that even though we know exactly what the Past was objectively, we cannot know the truth of it any better than Hugo. The significant use of time in *Dirty Hands* lies in the critical instant at which Hugo realizes that he literally does not know why he shot Hoederer—back there years ago—but that this does not matter in any case. The important thing is that he must at this instant choose the present meaning of the Past and that his decision is the choice of a Future as well. His life literally depends on what he declares the Past to have been.

Since Hugo himself was unable to determine retrospectively and with certainty his precise motives at the time of the shooting, it is hardly legitimate for the critic to seek a final answer. We may quite appropriately inquire, as Hugo did, concerning his emotional state at that time, and we can try to understand what prevented him from knowing how to answer truthfully when questioned. When the usually overreflective Hugo finally pulled the trigger, he was acting wholly nonreflectively, in "the emotional mode." We can be reasonably sure that jealousy was there, but jealousy of whom? We have been led to believe that neither love nor true respect existed between Hugo and the elegant young wife, Jessica, who could not keep from laughing when he made love to her. Yet he may have felt possessive of her. Hoederer, in direct reference to Jessica, had remarked scornfully that Hugo, like other rich young intellectuals, brought their baggage with them when they crossed class lines. Hugo may well have been jealous of Hoederer's ability to win a kind of response from Jessica which he himself could not achieve. He may also have been jealous not of, but on account of, Hoederer. I do not suggest that there were homosexual implications. Nevertheless, Hugo declares that he had loved Hoederer, and his actions bear out this fact. He may well have resented Hoederer's turning his attentions to Jessica at a time when Hugo's own relations with him were at a moment of crisis. Hurt pride was certainly present. Hugo felt dimly that he had been made a fool of. For a moment it occurred to him that Hoederer's offer of alliance might have been for the purpose of keeping Jessica on the scene. During the preceding days, he had been convinced that Hoederer was a traitor to the party. To find that Hoederer was a small-time deceiver suggested that his earlier defense of his position might have been nothing but lies. Finally, Hugo's sense of being slighted as a husband is closely allied to the feeling that until now nobody has really believed in him as a man of action. By shooting Hoederer, he proves that he has carried out the mission which had been somewhat grudgingly entrusted to him.

What, then, finally made Hugo shoot? There are two reasons why he cannot answer with any certainty. His action was nonreflective. This does not mean that he was unaware of his emotions when he acted; there is no question of an unconscious here. If at the critical moment someone could have arrested his hand long enough to ask him why and force him to reflect, he would have come to "know" his motives. The resultant analysis might have ended by his shooting or by his resolving not to shoot, but at least he would have known later what his reasons had been. As it is, his emotional state at the time of the action was dimly comprehended by Hugo but not *known*. Since he did not reflect on it then, there is no *knowledge* to be remembered. Hugo's later reflection may attempt to judge the weight of those earlier motives, but it is no longer a consciousness with the same point of view. An unbridgeable nothingness stands between Hugo's present consciousness and his past.

The second explanation of why he cannot say what made him kill Hoederer is found in Sartre's theory of emotions as presented in his 1939 essay *Esquisse d'une Théorie des Emotions* (*The Emotions: Outline of a Theory*). Since the time of Homer, when deities were invoked to explain nonrational impulses, psychologists have tended to think of emotions as forces which sweep over man and drive him to action. They are opaque, all but material, and function somehow like invaders of the psyche rather than as a structure or activity of the psyche itself. Emotions have been offered as excuses for action, as though a person might be overcome by love or hate or fear as by an external force. Sartre insists that emotion is a mode of consciousness, a purposive conduct. In contrast with perception, which aims at the real, and with imagination, which introduces the unreal, the emotional consciousness posits the real world as its object, but transforms the world by altering its own connections with the world, living as if the world and its potentialities were governed by laws of magic. Emotion is magical behavior and uses the body as its means of incantation. In emotion the body, "directed by consciousness, changes its relations with the world in order that the world may change its qualities." [5]

In illustrating his view of emotion as purposeful conduct, Sartre uses such examples as the following: A girl is trying to confess a painful incident to a psychiatrist; she is so overcome by sobbing that she cannot continue. This is the ordinary way of stating what happened. Sartre argues that we might more accurately say that she sobs emotionally *in order that* she might not be obliged to continue. Or a man arguing a philosophical point with an opponent sees that he is trapped. He alters the situation by becoming so angry that he calls his opponent names and presents the whole idea of debate as ridiculous. Or a woman crosses between a bear and her cubs and sees the animal charging her. Unable to see any means of escape, she faints from fear, thereby annihilating the bear in her consciousness since she cannot cope with the real situation. Even joy, Sartre argues, involves mimetic bodily activity. If I receive a piece of good news recognizing some past achievement or promising me a great happiness in the future, I may jump up and down, raise my voice and shout, clap my hands—all ways of endeavoring to realize magically right

[5] *The Emotions: Outline of a Theory*, translated by Bernard Frechtman (New York: Philosophical Library, 1948), p. 61.

now all the fulfillment which will be realized realistically only over a long period of time and in a multitude of acts. In all these examples we see that emotion is ineffective. One's personal relation to the world is changed but not the world itself.

I mention this view of emotion in connection with Hugo's decision because I think both the weakness and the strength of the theory may be seen in this example. The weakness seems to me to lie in Sartre's insistence on the word "magical." In the examples just given, it was easy to see that the change in consciousness affected only the person himself. But when Hugo shot Hoederer, the body so drastically modified was not Hugo's but Hoederer's. What seems to be lacking, or at least not spelled out, is the connection between the magical or mimetic activity and real action in the world. Of course, this is probably exactly the distinction Sartre is making. So long as consciousness remains in the emotional mode, its conduct is without real effect outside itself, though even here, of course, one cannot discount the effect my emotion may have on another subject who witnesses it. The choice to act directly on the world is not the same as the emotion which accompanies the action.

If this distinction appears somewhat tenuous, the other aspect of Sartre's theory—that emotions are chosen modes of behavior rather than compelling forces—seems to fit Hugo's case very well. We have tried to analyze some of the ingredients of his emotional state when he committed the crime, but in a sense our very analysis was a falsification. It resembles a procedure to which Sartre has specifically objected, particularly as it has been demonstrated in the work of Proust. We have catalogued the various feelings as if they existed there in Hugo's psyche like so many layers or like proportions of un-mixed chemical ingredients. Sartre would object on two scores. First, if I feel toward someone a friendship tinged with hostility, my feeling is not a combination of the two or a fluctuation from one to another but a new feeling which is neither friendship nor hostility. Even when I am aware of it as friendliness, it is a friend-liness which would not be the same if the hostility were not, so to speak, waiting there on the horizon. If love and hate are present together, says Sartre, the result might be compared with coffee thoroughly mixed with cream but not to pure coffee with a layer of cream on top. More important, emotions are ways in which we relate ourselves to objects, including people and my own psychic object; they do not come to us from out-side. Hugo, faced with various possibilities of interpret-ing and modifying the situation in which he found him-self, chose to perform the one act which altered it ir-reparably and at once rather than to explore and to choose reflectively between the consequences to be ef-fected by one course of action rather than another. It is a terrifying example of the freedom to cut ourselves off from a considered responsibility for past and future; it was not an act determined by any identifiable emotion or combination of emotions which overcame the will. It is interesting that Hugo at no point tries to excuse or to justify himself by appeal to overpowering emotion. He does not say that he "was not himself" when he shot Hoederer. He accepts full responsibility for the murder. Yet he remarks that his crime seems strangely light, to possess no weight, to be nothing at all except what he chooses to make it. I find here a curious parallel (despite obvious differences) with the famous murder in Camus's

The Stranger, which Meursault can explain only by saying, "It was because of the sun."

Abandoning all hope of pinning down forever the Past as it was, Hugo finally says that he does not know why he killed Hoederer, but he does know now why it was right to kill him. Simultaneously remaking the Past and choosing the Future, he announces, "I have not yet killed Hoederer, Olga. Not yet. But I am going to kill him now, along with myself." The answer which he gives ensures his death. The reasons for it, while arrived at by clear reflection, are almost as complex and contradictory as those surrounding the former act. By refusing to say that Hoederer was "killed over a woman," Hugo will give him "the death he deserves." At the same time, he declares that it was right to kill Hoederer because his policy was wrong, because he lied to the party members, and because his action was imperiling the life of the party. Furthermore, if Hugo chose to live now, he would be working for a party which had adopted Hoederer's line after having ordered him murdered.

Hugo's willingness to die for the sake of ennobling the reputation of a man he believes to have been wrong is but one of the things which have left audiences doubtful as to the correct interpretation of the play. Personally, I think that the difficulty of arriving at an easy judgment as to whether Hugo was right or wrong, whether he or Hoederer is "the real hero," whether the play is pro- or anti-Communist testifies to its artistic merit and its author's honesty rather than to any literary obscurity. There is much ambivalence, but it is not the unintentional ambiguity which comes from unclear writing. Comments made by Sartre and reported by de

Beauvoir would have us believe that *Dirty Hands* was not intended as a political play at all. Sartre claims to have been interested simply in exploring the character and situation of a bourgeois intellectual who sincerely devotes himself to working for the Communists but whose intellectual habits and thought patterns alienate him from his fellow workers. De Beauvoir writes,

He had imagined a character who would be a young Communist, born into the bourgeoisie, seeking to erase his origins by means of an act, but incapable of wrenching himself free from his subjectivity, even at the price of an assassination. Set in opposition to him was a militant party leader totally devoted to his objectives.[6]

Granted that this was Sartre's original intention, it is hard to accept his claim that the completed play had no political implications. Certainly the internal struggles of the Proletarian Party in Illyria resembled those of the Communist Party which all of Europe had recently witnessed. De Beauvoir admits this when she says that the party's reversal after the death of the man it killed was

politically the most truthful moment in the play: in Communist Parties all over the world, when an opposition group attempts to force the adoption of a new and justified policy, it is liquidated (with or without physical violence); then those in control take over the suggested change and adapt it to their own purposes. [p. 168]

It seems hardly possible that Sartre intended to condone such procedure. It is true, however, that he has consistently maintained that *Dirty Hands* is not anti-Com-

[6] *La Force des choses*, p. 166.

munist, and de Beauvoir goes so far as to suggest that those who found it so were reading into it their own prejudices:

In the case of Illyria—inspired by Hungary—the Party's hesitations and its final decision were justified by the circumstances; but here its internal difficulties were exposed to people who were looking at it from the outside with animosity. They gave to the play the meaning which it did in fact have for them. This is why Sartre refused on several occasions to let it be performed outside France.

The history of *Dirty Hands* since its first performance illustrates the way in which the World "steals my action from me." Dramatically the play was an instant success with its audience. Establishment critics withheld their final judgment until the Communist papers attacked Sartre as having sold out to America. Then, de Beauvoir reports, "the bourgeoisie immediately buried Sartre in bouquets." Once, "during a thaw," the play was performed in Yugoslavia. In New York it was highly successful but under circumstances which angered Sartre considerably. The title was changed to *Red Gloves*, a highly significant alteration. Hoederer at one point taunts Hugo, accusing him of being all too willing to wear the red gloves of bloodshed but too fastidious to get his hands dirty in the compromises of realistic politics. The title, the direction, and slight shifts of emphasis in the dialogue made Hugo unmistakably the sympathetic hero of the play, especially for an audience predisposed to see it as anti-Communist. Yet Sartre has stated explicitly and on more than one occasion that in his opinion it was Hoederer who was right.

In the long run, what is more interesting than the

problem of Sartre's attitude toward the Communists in 1948 is the specific nature of the conflict between Hugo and Hoederer. It revolves around the same issue as the unfortunate debate between Sartre and Camus several years later: the relation between ends and means, between principle and political necessity. Although it is easy to see that subsequent events vindicate Hoederer so far as his specific course of action is concerned, any attempt to defend his position when it is formulated abstractly runs into difficulties. In so many words he states that "all means are good when they are effective." He is not merely willing to compromise with his opponents, which in itself is not necessarily bad since Hoederer dictated terms advantageous to his own side, but he has no scruples about lying to the people whose interests he is representing. Hugo raises the pertinent question as to whether a party which uses exactly the same methods as its opponents is any more worthy of support than they are. Moreover, Hoederer acts absolutely on the basis of his own view of the situation, without authority, playing God because he is sure he is right. So far as his constituents are concerned, he might as well be a dictator. This attitude is disturbing, to say the least, and we can certainly understand why many in the audience have felt that regardless of Hoederer's attractive personal qualities and his correctness in the immediate situation, Hugo was right to condemn his policy.

On the other hand, Hugo's position, although irreproachable in principle, does not bear up under analysis. He stands for honesty and integrity, for refusal to sacrifice principle for mere expediency; but it is the kind of adherence to principle which is life-destroying. When Hoederer points out to him that in the present crisis, a compromise with principle will not only ultimately benefit the party but will save thousands of human lives, Hugo shows himself willing to sacrifice living individuals for theoretical purity. "You can't make a revolution with flowers." He defends this too easy acceptance of bloodshed with the statement that he is looking toward the future, that he loves men for what they may become. Hoederer retorts that he loves them for what they are. Suddenly Hugo is seen to be a not too distant relative of the Autodidacte, the false humanist who loved mankind out of empty sentimentality. Still Hugo's final decision to die so that Hoederer might have the life he deserved, while it may smack of romanticism, does show him capable of heroic action.

There is one other suggestion that Sartre is not weighting the scales wholly on Hoederer's side. This is his use of the symbolism of lightness and heaviness. We have noted that Hugo felt that his crime was curiously light. Before the murder, he had remarked that he felt himself to be without weight, that there were a heaviness and solidity about Hoederer that made other things seem real when he touched them. If we considered this play alone, we might tend to interpret these words as simply contributing to Hoederer's maturity and self-confidence as contrasted with the immature and vacillating Hugo. But we have observed that in *Bariona* Sartre equated this sense of lightness with the realization of human freedom. The same symbolism occurs elsewhere. It is almost a major theme in the short story "Childhood of a Leader," where the young Lucien longs for, and ultimately achieves, the heavy, stonelike solidity of self-righteous bourgeois adults—such as "the stinkers" in the picture gallery. He takes up anti-Semitism as well, and Sartre's portrait of the anti-Semite in *Anti-Semite and*

Jew stresses again the heavy impermeability the anti-Semite shares with the rock. It seems unlikely that the symbolic use of lightness and heaviness in *Dirty Hands* does not still hold some of these same connotations. If Sartre has put into the portrait of Hugo certain ironic references to himself as a highly subjective, existentialist intellectual trying to work with the Communists while not ever becoming one of them, I think that the picture of the party member Hoederer has not been given to us without certain slight thrusts at the unquestioning sureness with which he pursues his objectives.

It is possible to see in *Dirty Hands* both echoes and anticipations. The play reflects the troubles Sartre was already encountering in trying to cooperate with the Communists. Just a few months later his efforts to form a politically effective coalition of all Leftist parties failed largely because of Communist intransigence. The play also looks forward to the period of the early fifties when Sartre came to believe that the sole hope for social progress in France lay in working actively with the Communists as the only ones who held the interests of the workers at heart. It was in 1952 that he proclaimed over the radio that anyone who declared his wish to work with the Communists without being willing to become a member and submit himself to party discipline was—like himself—"a slimy rat." In *Dirty Hands* perhaps we can see both why Sartre would make such a statement and why, despite this proclamation, he himself never became a member of the Communist party.

Finally, the play gives us a glimpse into a more positive view of personal human relations than we have observed up till now. The picture of individuals acting and judging their acts by their own private value systems was never clearer. Hugo's final decision would almost certainly not have won Hoederer's approval. One can almost hear the latter complaining that Hugo's chosen death was so much idealistic nonsense, that if Hugo really wanted to serve mankind, he might much better forget the past and his private disagreements and live to work in the party ranks. The fact remains that Hugo dies for the sake of honoring the memory of a man whose value system he could not accept for himself. And Hoederer risked his life for Hugo. For no reason other than wanting to help Hugo, he deliberately allowed Hugo to pull the gun on him although he had been warned by Jessica that Hugo intended to shoot. At the end Hoederer's last words—a lie at that—are an attempt to save Hugo. He tells his party bodyguards not to hurt Hugo, that the latter had shot Hoederer out of justifiable anger since Hoederer had been sleeping with his wife. It is hardly going too far to say that each man died for the other.

The Condemned of Altona

Sartre's last play was *Les Séquestrés d'Altona* (produced in 1959, published in 1960; *The Condemned of Altona*, 1960), which may be said to present in new combination many of the things we have seen in the examples chosen for discussion. Like *Dirty Hands*, it is built around a man's attempt to cope with his past—this time in an endeavor to escape it and in bad faith. The setting is realistic and contemporary, but, as in *Bariona*, the political problem of one time and place is used to mirror another. The German, Franz, who had directed the torture of prisoners in World War II, is used to appeal to the conscience of France, which had allowed the torture of Algerians by French paratroopers. Finally, Sartre himself has said of the play that it is "a *No Exit* with five characters."

Once again Sartre employs flashbacks, inserting into the stream of present action a series of brief scenes from the past. This time, unlike those in *No Exit*, the scenes are not described but enacted. The character who has referred to them participates in them, and the listening characters occasionally interrupt with comments. Clearly these reenactments are carefully limited to what the narrator wants the others to know, though there is no falsification in what is actually shown. In this play more than in any other of Sartre's, we are made aware of another dimension of Time, the future, represented by an imaginary Tribunal from the thirtieth century, which the mad Franz believes is constantly looking down on us and judging us.

In *The Condemned of Altona* the characters' final judgment on the meaning of their past is arrived at through a series of present confrontations. Herr von Gerlach, the wealthy owner of a shipbuilding firm, informs his daughter, his son, and his daughter-in-law that he is soon to die of cancer. He asks his son, Werner, to swear on the Bible that he will take over the business and that he will continue to live in the family home. Werner complies, and his wife, Johanna, is horrified, partly because she does not want to leave the life the two had been planning together in Hamburg and partly because she cannot bear to see her independent and rebellious young husband suddenly transformed into a cringing, obedient child, grateful to receive a trust from a father who had never respected or loved him. Johanna realizes that Werner is being sacrificed to his older brother, Franz, the father's favorite. The bare outline of Franz's story is told to her: In 1941 Franz, about eighteen years old, learned that his father had sold land to the Nazis for a concentration camp. Franz sheltered an escaped rabbi and informed his father that the prisoner was there in the house. Herr von Gerlach notified the authorities, the rabbi was captured and killed before Franz's eyes, and the father obtained pardon for his son on condition that he go into the army. When the war was over, Franz returned home. Father and son argued over the question of national guilt. Herr von Gerlach maintained that either the responsible leaders must be punished or the country as a whole must shoulder their crimes. Franz retorted that the people would be destroyed either way—by being condemned as a whole or by being forced to repudiate their leaders. He startled his father by claiming that all were innocent. Every one of the so-called German crimes was necessary, a justified means of opposing the greater crimes proposed by the con-quering Allies. "Was Goering the one who dropped the bomb on Hiroshima?" Franz claimed that what had been planned all along was the systematic extermination of the German people. A short time later he attacked and almost killed an American officer who, first led on and then taunted by Leni, Franz's sister, had tried to rape her. Once again the father successfully used his influence to get Franz off, this time on condition that he leave the country for South America. Franz refused to go and locked himself in a room upstairs, where he has remained for thirteen years without seeing anyone but Leni. If he should be discovered now, he would be arrested.

In a scene between Franz and Leni which follows shortly after this account, we learn that Franz has re-treated into madness. Supposedly he stays sequestered because he cannot bear to see the suffering of the Ger-man victims. Quite obviously the real reason is that he does not want to see the prosperity of a restored Germany, which would destroy any justification for what he, as a German officer under the Nazis, had done. His delirium is protected by Leni, who conceals all real information from him and nourishes his delusion with false tales of atrocities perpetrated against the German people.

Franz's flimsy defense is destroyed. The father makes a secret pact with Johanna: He will reveal to her the secret knock to which Franz will open. (The father knows it from having spied on Leni, though he has been afraid to use it himself.) If Johanna will tell Franz of his father's imminent death and his request for an interview with his son, Herr von Gerlach will release Werner from his promise to take over the firm. Johanna sees Franz several times. Like Leni she lies to him, partly out of pity and the fear that the truth might kill him, partly because of her own fascination for him. Leni learns of the situation and out of jealousy tells Franz the truth about postwar Germany and informs Johanna that Franz, far from being an innocent tool of the Nazis, had himself tortured Russian prisoners. Johanna turns from him in revulsion. Franz leaves his room and talks with his father. In a bitterly painful interview, the two condemn each other even as they are able to understand and to love each other. They leave together with the intention of driving a car over the cliff in a double suicide. Johanna departs with Werner. Leni goes to replace Franz as voluntary prisoner in the room upstairs.

The Condemned of Altona is so rich in Sartrean themes that a full discussion of it might by itself serve as a fairly adequate introduction to Sartre. I wish here to concentrate on two things: the way in which the play, retrospectively, illustrates Sartre's views of human relations and individual psychology, and the way in which, prospectively, its view of man and history lead toward the *Critique*.

On the personal level, the Look is more metaphorical than in *No Exit*; the pattern of interpersonal relations is richer and more complex but not essentially changed. It is the Look of the father which shows Johanna that her relation with Werner had been for each of them an attempt to escape rather than a union based on mutual appreciation. Her realization of this truth is further strengthened by Leni's pointed remark that "some marriages are funerals." The appearance of Johanna brings to an end the incestuous relationship which had existed between Franz and Leni. The disintegrating power of the Third is demonstrated still more clearly by Leni's choice to make both Franz and Johanna see each other with different eyes. And we may say that the father, who anticipated what would happen, was using everyone as an object for his own purpose. Franz's relation with each of the women shows patterns which we have seen before. With Johanna it is almost a *folie à deux*. A former cinema star who had just failed to reach the top, she had married Werner partly to conceal her failure. More than that, she abandoned her career out of frustration. For Johanna, her acting was for the sake of capturing herself on the screen, but she could never succeed in coinciding with the image; she could not find in her likeness the Johanna which other people saw. What fascinates her in Franz is his declaration that he will bear witness to all eternity that she is beautiful. Although she never really believes in his imaginary Tribunal, the fact that he does gives to her the sense of *being* the objective self she has chosen for the Other to see—forever. For Franz, of course, she provides the objective support he needs for his delirium. The relation is a travesty on the project of love which Sartre has described in *Being and Nothingness*.

With Leni we see other patterns of bad faith. Leni wants Franz out of pride, because she "can give herself only to a Gerlach." We feel that her willingness to sustain his illusions is not entirely out of either pity or passion. So long as he remains unawakened, he is her object. At one point she does plead with him indirectly to cease defending himself and to acknowledge what he is without apology. She is willing to accept him as confessed torturer. But this does not mean that in the true sense she understands and feels with him. It is, rather, that she does not have the horror for his crimes that he himself feels. This is the only example of overtly incestuous love between brother and sister which Sartre has developed, but he has hinted at the theme elsewhere. There is the pair of young Russians in *The Roads to Freedom*, and there are Orestes and Electra in *The Flies*. The recognition scene between the second two reads like one of the tenderest of love scenes, and we feel that only Electra's later failure to live up to her promise prevented its fulfillment as a complete adult union. Sartre himself has commented that the one family relationship which moves him is that between brother and sister. He explains it partly by the fact that his mother, being treated by her father as if she were a child herself, seemed to Sartre like an older sister. He adds that he longed to have a younger sister, too, and remarks, "I have often committed the serious mistake of seeking in women that sister who never existed." That all of this remained a whimsical sort of fantasy is borne out by a footnote which perhaps explains why in the one case where the wish-fulfillment is dramatically actualized, Sartre chose so unattractive a sister as Leni. "What attracted me in this family bond was less the erotic temptation than the prohibition against making love: fire and ice, mingled delights and frustration, incest pleased me so long as it remained platonic." [7]

Franz's madness is of particular interest to us in its relation to Sartre's view of psychoanalysis. Franz spends his time making "speeches for the defense," which he imagines that he as defending attorney is delivering before a Tribunal of the thirtieth century which is composed of crabs. Sometimes he speaks directly to the ceiling where presumably the Crabs are watching; sometimes he talks into a tape recorder, still further emphasizing that the address is to posterity. On other occasions, he grinds oyster shells against each other, particularly when he is trying to escape the presence of a witness from the real world (Leni or Johanna), or to avoid the attention of the Crabs after he has said something "dangerous," or to avoid thinking out things too clearly in his own mind. The marine imagery is not only appropriate to the situation but revealing of Sartre's own preoccupations. The oyster, of course, is an obvious symbol of sequestration, of withdrawing into one's shell. We have already observed the presence of shellfish in Sartre's mescaline hallucinations. Roquentin, in *Nausea*, feared that if he watched a hand, it might suddenly transform itself into a monstrous crab. Until the publication of *The Words*, I had always imagined that the Tribunal of Crabs might have been inspired by H. G. Wells's picture of the last earthly inhabitants in *The Time Machine*, and this may indeed have suggested to Sartre the idea of representing crabs as all that were left in the thirtieth century. But again there is a relevant passage in Sartre's autobiography.

The child Sartre saw one day a picture of a moonlit

[7] *Les Mots*, pp. 41–42.

quay where a huge, gnarled claw reached out of the water to drag a man down into its depths. The caption read, "Was it a drunkard's hallucination? Did Hell open up?" The child was horribly frightened by the picture, but he derived from it inspiration for his own adventure stories. He wrote of heroes who suddenly confronted a gigantic octopus with flaming eyes, a twenty-ton crustacean, a monstrous talking spider. Significantly, he never finished these episodes; the hero was neither handed over to "the Beast" nor allowed to overcome it. Sartre left a couple of pages blank and took up again with new adventures. He claims that each of these monsters was a projection of himself. "It was myself, the child monster; it was my boredom with living, my fear of dying, my mawkishness, and my perversity" (p. 126).

We may choose here. We may, if we like, see these images as purely private symbols which have remained consistent for Sartre throughout his lifetime. Both in his personal experiences and in his writing, mollusks and shellfish stand for the hidden threat lurking beneath the surface. Sometimes, as in *Nausea*, they represent the terrifying, pointless emergence of the nonhuman in an irrational universe. More often they are a projection of the anxieties of an unauthentic or unfulfilling life. Alternatively, we may, consistently with Sartre's own psychological theory, take the position that objects in the world manifest certain objective qualities of existence and that we can hope to understand a person by observing how he has chosen to relate himself to these objects. Sartre's most famous example is his brilliant description of slime, "the agony of water," the not quite liquid and not yet solid, the surreptitious which dares not speak its name. Slime stands for the great Anti-Value, the opposite of the In-itself-for-itself. It represents the state of a For-itself which would know itself to be an enslaved, paralyzed freedom. For Sartre, the analogy between slime as a physical substance and a slimy handshake or a slimy person is more than metaphor. It involves the perception of likeness. It is, I suppose, what we mean by a "natural symbol."

We must be careful here, for Sartre explicitly rejects what he calls Freud's "universal pansymbolism" in which an object has an unchanging reference which we can interpret as if we were translating a language—for example, a pincushion = a woman's breast, or gold = the feces. Whether or not Sartre's symbolism is as altogether different from Freud's as he believes is a serious question. In the case of the sea creatures, however, their suggestion of a threat coming from somewhere in the hidden depths seems natural. One may recall the marine imagery which Eliot uses in "The Love Song of J. Alfred Prufrock" to express the subterranean life of the buried, half-paralyzed Self.

The scenes in Franz's room are especially interesting in connection with Sartre's statement that "we choose our psychoses." While this way of putting it may be offensive to some psychiatrists, most would agree that psychosis is a way of retreating from reality and at the same time a technique for coping with it. Although the device of physical sequestration is a bit more obvious than in the usual case, Franz's refusal to see the outside world as it is in order to sustain the illusion that it is what he wants it to be is just another way of saying that he has chosen the private, emotional (Sartre would say magical) way of relating himself to the world instead of the rational one. His self-seclusion and his will not to see the truth are not by themselves sufficient to punish and at the same time to assuage his guilt feelings.

The invention of the Tribunal of Crabs accomplishes exactly this feat. By assuming that our whole century is on trial and that he is its defender, Franz is constantly called on to deal with his guilt but in a controlled situation in which absolution is always possible so long as the final sentence has not been pronounced. Significantly, Franz fluctuates between controlling his "delirium" to the point of knowing when it is threatened and being helplessly imprisoned by it. This situation is familiar in the annals of psychiatry. If the process appears here rather too obvious to be wholly credible—except by willing suspension of disbelief—this is only partly the result of dramatic requirements. It is also because Sartre is stressing what separates him from the Freudian tradition more radically than anything else: his denial of the Unconscious. We can see that Sartre's theory · ould not allow him to postulate a region of the psyche with contents which on principle are hidden from consciousness. Consciousness possesses no contents; it is translucent process. But because it is both reflective and nonreflective, the For-itself can lie to itself; it can be in bad faith.

In *Being and Nothingness*, Sartre offered a fairly lengthy criticism of the Freudian concept of the Unconscious. He claimed that once having broken the psychic unity, the Freudian can no longer account for such things as the symbolic satisfaction of repressed desires, or the resistance which the patient offers when the unconscious material is about to be brought to light by the psychoanalyst, or the purposive function of dreams. He argued that what Freud has done is to introduce at the level of the Censor the phenomenon of bad faith which his theory of consciousness cannot explain. We shall see that later Sartre himself came to recognize the necessity of allowing for a certain opaque irrationality in the existential choice of being, thus modifying it to the point that he felt it best to introduce a new term, *le vécu* or the lived experience. In *Being and Nothingness,* even the psychotic consciousness reacts by rational principles or at least along lines which can be rationally interpreted. But we must not underestimate the subtlety of his early "existential psychoanalysis." Much of the time when we say of ourselves that we did or felt something unconsciously, we actually mean nonreflectively. Already in *The Psychology of Imagination* Sartre had recognized that in our imagining, having introduced the unreal, we may allow ourselves to become so fascinated with the unreal images that return to the everyday world is difficult. In the case of Franz, we do not need reference to unconscious motivation to explain his original retreat from reality or the particular quality of his psychosis or his final emergence from it.

There are other significant symbols in the play. At one point Franz suddenly pulls off one of the medals from his uniform and eats it. It is made of chocolate, and this suggests another important aspect of these scenes. They raise again the old question as to what is true and real. The chocolate medals are not real medals, on one level. Yet symbolically they are a truer expression of military values than genuine ones would be. Thirtieth-century crabs are not physically in the room, but the realization that our acts will be judged by the future which we help to make—this awareness is truly present to Franz's consciousness and to our own.

In *The Condemned of Altona,* Sartre's last play, as in *Bariona,* his first, Sartre ends with a direct address to the audience. The stage is bare except for a tape recorder on which Leni has just put Franz's "best speech for the defense."

The century would have been a good one if man had not

been struck down by his cruel, immemorial enemy, by the flesh-eating species which had vowed his destruction, by the hairless, malignant beast—by man. The beast was hiding, we surprised his look suddenly in the depths of our neighbors' eyes. Then we struck—legitimate self-defense. I surprised the beast. I struck, a man fell. In his dying eyes I saw the beast still alive, myself. . . . From whom, from what do I find this dull rancid taste in my mouth? From man? From the beast? From myself. It is the taste of the century. . . . (*Pause. Turns to the Crabs.*) The century is a woman in labor. Will you condemn your mother. Answer! (*Pause.*) The thirtieth century no longer replies. Perhaps there will be no more centuries after ours. Perhaps a bomb will blow out all the lights. Everything will be dead: eyes, judges, time. Night. Oh, Tribunal of the Night, I, Franz von Gerlach, here in this room, have taken the century upon my shoulders and have said, I will answer for it. This day and for ever. What do you say? [8]

The "you" in the last sentence is each one of us and all of us. We may call it the Look of History. Sartre has commented, "I wanted the spectator to feel himself to some degree in the presence of this tribunal. . . . Or, quite simply, in the presence of centuries to come." [9]

We see in the quoted passage another reference to that Beast which is inside us, which is oneself and which nevertheless sets up an objective situation in which we find ourselves trapped. Franz seems to refer to his discovery within himself of the capacity for pleasure in cruelty, of sadism. Possibly we should find here only a reference to that basic conflict of subjects and object

[8] *Les Séquestrés d'Altona* (Paris: Gallimard, 1960).

[9] Sartre made this statement in an interview with representatives of *L'Express*, sections of which have been published under the title "The Theater," translated by Richard Seaver. *Evergreen Review* (January-February, 1960), pp. 143–52.

which we have already discussed, but it is tempting to see in it a wider reference and an anticipation of a basic theme in the *Critique*, which Sartre was completing during the same period in which he wrote *The Condemned of Altona*. Until now, Sartre says, the human race has lived in a milieu of scarcity. There is simply not enough of what we need for us all to survive. Thus by his very existence, each man assumes a dimension which is nonhuman. He is potentially a bringer of death to the Other.

Nothing—neither wild beasts nor microbes—can be more terrible for man than a cruel, intelligent, flesh-eating species which could understand and thwart human intelligence and whose aim would be precisely the destruction of man. This species is obviously our own . . . in the milieu of scarcity. [p. 208]

Capitalism has grown up as an institution to enable some men to cope with this situation by reducing others to submen, to objects, or by declaring them expendable. But by now the system itself has proved to be the winner; employers and employees are equally its slaves. Herr von Gerlach realizes that his firm has become too big for any owner. It runs itself, recruits its own managers. He himself is "a hat on a flagpole." He pays his employee "to tell him what orders to give." The milieu of scarcity has assumed the form of a field of worked-over matter in which I am alienated from myself. Man has become the product of his product. We can see now why Sartre felt it necessary to reinterpret the meaning of *No Exit*. In the *Critique*, "Hell is the *pratico-inerte*." Hell is the situation which others have set up for me. Hell is the world into which I was born, and it is where I must live.

7

HELL IS THE OUTSIDE WORLD

Seventeen years separate *Being and Nothingness* (1943) from the *Critique* (1960).[1] The *Critique* may be properly called a Neo-Marxist work. Some critics, both non-Communist and (more rarely) Communist, claim that it is Marxism pure and simple, by which they mean that its author is no longer an existentialist. In so doing, they ignore explicit statements by Sartre himself. In "Search for a Method," an essay which precedes the *Critique* proper,[2] Sartre claims that there is in any given era only one philosophy which adequately expresses the general movement of society. For our time it is Marxism. Existentialism is an ideology which lives parasitically on the margin of Marxism. It is a vitally necessary ideology if Marxism is to be freed from its present ossified state and allowed to continue its growth. "The autonomy of existential studies results necessarily from the negative qualities of Marxists and not from Marxism itself" (p. 181).

In describing his first discovery of Marxism when he was a student, Sartre says,

We were convinced *at one and the same time* that historical materialism furnished the only valid interpretation of his-

[1] Original publication dates.

[2] This is the only section of the *Critique* which has appeared in English except for brief selections in anthologies. *Search for a Method*, translated by Hazel E. Barnes (New York: Alfred A. Knopf, 1963).

tory and that existentialism remained the only concrete
approach to reality. I do not pretend to deny the contradictions in this attitude. . . . . Many intellectuals, many
students, have lived and still live with the tension of this
double demand. How does this come about? . . . Marxism,
after drawing us to it as the moon draws the tides, after transforming all our ideas, after liquidating the categories of
our bourgeois thought, abruptly left us stranded. It did not
satisfy our need to understand. In the particular situation in
which we were placed, it no longer had anything new to
teach us, because it had come to a stop. [p. 21]

There has been a recent attempt to explain the link
between existentialist and Marxist thought as the result
of the rediscovery of the very early works of Marx. It
is true that Sartre has been interested in these works and
true also that he tends to criticize Engels and, even
more, contemporary Marxists for distorting what Marx
himself proposed. Yet it would be mistaken to see in
Sartre's arguments only an attempt to return to the
source—like that of certain religious groups which claim
to have rediscovered Christ beneath Christianity. Sartre's
criticism of traditional Marxism is not that it has been
allowed to follow a natural course of development but
that its growth has been arrested. Marxism began as a
dialectical interpretation of history, a theory of history
which in its very expression became a force in history. At
the hands of twentieth-century Marxists, dialectical materialism has become a carapace. They forcibly squeeze
historical events into a premanufactured interpretation
regardless of the violence which must be done to the
facts. Philosophical truth takes precedence over historical
truth. As a result, Marxism, which started out as a
movement to liberate man from his alienation, has become "a dialectic without men," has excluded man from

its considerations. The task of existentialism, says Sartre, is to revitalize Marxism by reinserting into it a concern with living men and women and children. Agreeing with Engels that men make history within determined conditions, Sartre reminds us that it is still men who make their history. At the moment it is existentialism, not Marxism, which seeks to relate the discoveries of a dynamic psychology and sociology to the interpretation of historical process. But the aim is to enable Marxism to become a living philosophy once again. Sartre concludes his essay with these words:

From the day that Marxist thought will have taken on the human dimension (that is, the existential project) as the foundation of anthropological Knowledge, existentialism will no longer have any reason for being. Absorbed, surpassed and conserved by the totalizing movement of philosophy, it will cease to be a particular inquiry and will become the foundation of all inquiry. The comments which we have made in the course of the present essay are directed—within the modest limit of our capabilities—toward hastening the moment of that dissolution.

If this Neo-Marxism is to be brought into existence as the result of absorbing the insights of existentialism and being modified by them, one can hardly say fairly that Sartre has currently abandoned existentialism or that he finds it irreconcilable with Marxism.

As early as 1946, Sartre published an article, "Materialism and Revolution," which, retrospectively at least, seems to suggest that sooner or later Sartre would undertake something comparable to what he in fact did undertake in the *Critique*. This essay has usually been considered to be his sharpest attack on Marxism. It is true that in it Sartre makes some biting criticisms and that he seems to be doing so from outside, certainly not as a writer who would someday declare that Marxism is "the only philosophy of our time." In the *Critique* Sartre refers to this article and acknowledges that he had been justly reproached by a critic who pointed out that Sartre had not even mentioned Marx's fundamental definition of materialism, one which Sartre himself adopts as basic to his later position: "The mode of production of material life generally dominates the development of social, political, and intellectual life." Sartre explains the omission as resulting from his having directed his criticisms primarily against Engels and the French Communists rather than against Marx. But he certainly had not specifically exempted Marx from his general criticisms of Marxism.

Three points are of primary importance to our discussion. First, the criticisms which Sartre makes of Marxism are essentially those he will make fourteen years later: Dialectical materialism has become entirely a dialectic of nature and not of human relations in history. Its economic laws function like laws of nature; human freedom is ignored. Revolution comes about as the result of impersonal forces rather than as the result of the awakening of free men and women to the fact of their alienation and oppression. Yet no given state of the world, says Sartre, can by itself produce class consciousness. Furthermore, Marxism has no metaphysical theory to explain the materialism and the view of nature on which its theory depends. Sartre's *Critique*, with its analysis of human praxis in the pratico-inerte, attempts to correct these deficiencies, though, I would contend, the basic ontology which serves as its philosophical foundation is still that of *Being and Nothingness*. A second point about the article is too often ignored. This is Sartre's insistence that the revolution which will overcome oppression and exploitation must originate with the working class and must aim at a classless society; in short, the statement of the essential goal is pure Marx. Third, Sartre, in the second half of the essay, presents his own requirements for the new revolutionary. Although not anti-Marxist, they go beyond traditional Marxism. I would argue that they represent a set of beliefs about the world which have remained unchanged in Sartre from his earliest writing until the present.

Sartre introduces this manifesto by the statement that we must realize that revolutionary action involves commitment to values. The revolutionary may distrust talk about values, as belonging to traditional idealist befuddlement. But insofar as he is acting in the name of a future order which he may not live to see but which serves to justify his present acts, this future serves as a value for him. "What is a value if not the call of something which does not yet exist?" Then Sartre states that a philosophy of revolution must replace the "materialist myth" by commitment to four principles: (1) Man is unjustifiable; his existence is contingent in that neither he himself nor Providence has brought it into being. (2) Consequently, any man-established collective order can be transcended toward another. (3) The current value system of any society reflects its structure and tends to preserve it. (4) This value system can be transcended toward another system which cannot presently be clearly discerned since the society which the new values will express does not yet exist; these values are foreshadowed and, indeed, invented by the very efforts to transcend the present society toward another.[3]

[3] "Matérialisme et révolution" was originally published in two parts in *Les Temps modernes* (June and July, 1946). In an English translation by Annette Michelson, it is included in a collection of articles by Sartre, *Literary and Philosophical Essays* (New York: Criterion Books, 1955). The section here discussed is found on pages 219–20.

Some of the problems of revolutions generally and certain of Sartre's own present difficulties may have their origin in the situation here formulated. Be that as it may, these four statements represent the nucleus of consistency in his career.

In the first assertion, that man's being is unjustifiable and contingent, we see the basis for Roquentin's anger at "the stinkers." It strikes at the heart of any notion of special right or privilege. It is as much against the claim that "the best shall rule" as it is opposed to aristocracies based on wealth or accident of birth. It cuts away any possibility of nonhuman or superhuman criteria by which one can prescribe in advance what man ought to be or by which one can assign to individuals their natural place. That any collective order may be transcended toward another follows logically. We must be careful to realize that this refers to more than the form of government, such as Democracy or Socialism. The collective order includes the whole structure of society with all its public and private institutions—the patterns of family life, for example, as well as forms of elections and official responsibilities. In claiming that value systems both reflect and perpetuate a social structure, Sartre is not precisely making Marx's claim that material conditions and modes of production dominate the social, political, and intellectual life, but the two statements are harmonious. Both recognize the inseparability of morals, concepts of the sacred, forms of human relations, and the prevailing economic and social institutions. Sartre goes even further than Marx in recognizing that to wipe out oppression and to destroy the class structure is to demand total resocialization. This would entail not only the reorganization of governmental, economic and educational institutions but also the restructuring of all patterns of social (including familial) relationships. It would include, of course, abolition of private property, at least in the form familiar to us.

The fourth point brings Sartre of 1946 side by side with militant revolutionaries of the late nineteen-sixties and early nineteen-seventies. It introduces what I should call "measured transcendence." One of the most frequently heard criticisms of today's young revolutionaries is that they want to tear down the existing order without having anything to put in its place. For the moment, I am not concerned with the justice or injustice of this reproach, but I think we can see why Sartre was predisposed to be sympathetic with those against whom it was leveled. If a revolutionary group is truly aiming at resocialization and not merely at the redistribution of existing goods and privileges, it will necessarily work to remove recognized evils without being able to anticipate in detail all that will be necessary to fill in the gap. To attempt a total theoretical reconstruction ahead of time would be to predetermine the new by experience limited to the old.

Sartre exhibits this same attitude toward measured transcendence in relation to his own thought and to the dialectical movement of philosophy and history. We have seen in the prefatory essay of the *Critique* his anticipation of the absorption of existentialism in an enriched and liberated Marxism. In the same way he predicts that Marxism, once it has accomplished its task, will be transcended by something else. The first step is to solve the problems of production so that man is not alienated in the structures which have been molded by scarcity. Then, "as soon as there will exist for *everyone* a margin of *real* freedom beyond the production of life, Marxism will have lived out its span; a philosophy of freedom will take its place. But we have no means, no intellectual instrument, no concrete experience which allows us to conceive of this freedom or of this philosophy." [p. 34] This quotation by itself demonstrates conclusively that when Sartre speaks of Marxism, he does not mean the totalitarian philosophy which is exemplified in any existing socialist nation. It shows, too, that he has not abandoned all belief in human freedom. The passage does indicate, however, that what interested him in 1960 was not the psychological freedom which is, for him, synonymous with human consciousness but rather the practical freedom which man needs to fulfill his projects in the world.

It is perhaps relevant here to comment on the fact that the "Ethics" which Sartre promised as a sequel to *Being and Nothingness* has never been written. Instead, we have the *Critique*. This is partly to be explained simply by Sartre's sense of priorities. His attitude is the reverse of that of would-be spiritual reformers, both Eastern and Western, who argue that the only way to improve society is to effect a change of heart in the individuals who make it up. Sartre and de Beauvoir both have argued that it is pointless, if not impossible, to work out an ethics for persons who must live in a society which is in bad faith. De Beauvoir even goes so far as to write that she and Sartre finally gave up authenticity.[4] All of this might well be debated on the theoretical level. On the practical side, we can easily see Sartre's point. If we have brought ourselves to accept, even provisionally, the basic fact that we live in a world whose institutions reflect oppression and injustice, any subsequent position, whether in act or in theory, is contaminated.

[4] *La Force des choses*, p. 122.

Where *Being and Nothingness* was concerned primarily with the process whereby consciousness internalizes its situation, the *Critique* examines those structures by which human freedom is alienated in the social environment. One of the collective devices by which freedom is ensnared is racism. It is illuminating to contrast two essays which Sartre wrote about racial prejudice, *Anti-Semite and Jew* (1946) and *Black Orpheus* (1948).[5] The movement from subjectivity to objectivity, from psychology to history is so clearly marked that it is hard to believe only two years separate their publication dates.

Anti-Semite and Jew is an erratically brilliant work. There are many statements in it to criticize. One wonders what strange lack of experience could have led Sartre to maintain that "we find scarcely any anti-Semitism among workers," or that anti-Semitism exists chiefly in the middle bourgeoisie since "the rich have better things to do." Despite a few specific references to dated events, the book seems almost to have been written in a historical vacuum. Significantly, Sartre indicates that for the anti-Semite, the Jew serves only as a pretext. "Elsewhere his counterpart will make use of the Negro or the man of yellow skin." Sartre's real object of analysis is not anti-Semitism as a historical phenomenon but the psychology of prejudice. He is probably correct but not original in claiming that racial prejudice derives from the neurotic need to feel that one possesses, by right of birth, an identifiable, inalienable value which makes one superior to at least some others. What is of primary interest to us is Sartre's attempt to explain the origin of the desire by relating it to his view of consciousness. Anti-Semitism is "fear of the human condition"; it is born of insecurity and anxiety. It is not

[5] Original publication dates.

an opinion but a passion. The anti-Semite is afraid of the demands of rationality and of the very nature of truth as "a thing of indefinite approximation." Or as Sartre says, "he longs for impenetrability." He does not want to feel that he makes himself but that he has been born already made, endowed with fixed qualities which make him, now and forever, what he is. In short, he flees from freedom and responsibility. Anti-Semitism is his device for bringing into existence the missing God. Obviously the anti-Semite is in bad faith; and because he is dimly aware of it, he rules in advance that his position is beyond argument, a given. As Sartre points out, prejudice is not based on experience but predefines the meaning of experience. He describes the gradual growth of such a person in the short story already mentioned, "Childhood of a Leader." We may note, however, that in the character of Lucien, anti-Semitism, though it is the final perfecting touch in his search for rocklike solidity, is not the central theme but a natural accompaniment to his fully formed bad faith. It is what Sartre has referred to as "secondhand anti-Semitism." Lucien, who has felt that he carried no weight with his friends, suddenly feels that he is endowed with an aggressive personality when he seizes the opportunity of making himself known and marked as "the man who hates Jews."

In the second part of *Anti-Semite and Jew*, Sartre raises the question of the authentic Jew. It is here that his subjective approach threatens almost to annihilate the Jew as a man who possesses a distinct cultural heritage. Sartre claims that the Gentile has created the Jew, and there is, of course, some truth in this assertion, just as we may say that the white man has created the "Negro problem." Yet Sartre's concepts of authenticity and unauthenticity for the Jew waver between accepting and rejecting assimilation as the goal. He associates un-authenticity with the notion of "universal man." The unauthentic Jew is playing the Gentile's game if he denies his "Jewishness." We must agree that to equate "Gentile" with human is wrong and dangerous as well as unauthentic; yet it seems that there is an authentic as well as an unauthentic way to strip away all racism from the idea of the "human." Sartre almost acknowledges this when he writes that the unauthentic Jew is an "indispensable leaven" in society because of "his rationalism, his critical spirit, his dream of a contractual society and of universal brotherhood, his humanism." [6] Still Sartre associates this judgment with the ideal of assimilation, which, he points out, the unauthentic Jew is willing to accept but not the anti-Semite. For the authentic Jew, Sartre can only suggest that he should embrace in angry pride the position which the anti-Semite has allotted him, that he proclaim and *will* his position as outcast. But Sartre admits that this position is socially ineffective. It may disarm the individual anti-Semite; it does not eradicate anti-Semitism. Sartre's only positive suggestion is for a "concrete liberalism" in which all races will be accepted equally, not because they all possess the same abstract human nature, but because, as participating citizens in the national enterprise, they have a right in that enterprise. "But they have these rights *as* Jews, Negroes, or Arabs—that is, as concrete persons." Sartre goes on to say that this goal can be accomplished only in a classless society, after total resocialization. Nobody should object to this ideal, but as Sartre presents it in his essay it remains vague and unattached to any concrete historical movement.

[6] *Anti-Semite and Jew*, translated by George J. Becker (New York: Grove Press, 1960), p. 146.

In sharp contrast with *Anti-Semite and Jew*, which reads like a postscript application of Sartre's early philosophy, *Black Orpheus* looks forward. It is concerned with analyzing a particular moment in the history of the blacks' struggle for liberation, and it represents Sartre's own active involvement in the conflict. *Black Orpheus* was written as an introduction to an anthology of poetry by black poets writing in French. The essay is concerned with the concept of "Negritude." Undoubtedly Sartre must have been influenced by things which he had read or heard from the blacks themselves, though he acknowledges no source other than the poems which he is introducing. Historically the essay has been influential in helping to crystallize and to formulate the blacks' own feeling about themselves. The editor of the anthology says of Sartre's preface that it is a "profoundly original study" which will "stand as a landmark in the analysis of Negritude." When the American translator of *Black Orpheus*, Samuel W. Allen, spoke in Denver in 1969, he presented his own discussion of Negritude in Sartrean terms, without in any way indicating that Sartre's "white" analysis was not entirely adequate and acceptable to him and to other black writers. In two ways this short work of Sartre's anticipates the author of the *Critique*. First, it attempts to pin down concretely the way in which the black finds himself a prisoner of a situation which others have made for him. Without denying that the black, like every other person, internalizes the situation within which he finds himself, Sartre tries to show how the very means by which a freedom makes itself have become for the black a process of alienation. Second, Sartre views the present stage of the struggle as part of a dialectical movement.

Although Sartre has maintained elsewhere that total

revolution must come from the working classes, he states here that the blacks have produced the only truly revolutionary poetry. The one way that the black can attain a sense of dignity as an individual is to affirm his solidarity with the blacks of all countries. It is obvious that the blacks have no one common language. Worse yet, a black has *no* language which does not serve to alienate him. In the *Critique* Sartre devotes considerable space to showing how language as such may cause my thought to deviate. Not only is there the obvious failure in communication because of variation in the connotations of words from one individual to another or from one period to another, but Sartre holds that our language reflects old habits of thought appropriate to an outmoded view of reality. Our concept of rationality must itself be modified if it is to fit the realities of our experience. In particular, he argues for the necessity of dialectical reason, which, unlike the analytical reason employed by science and mathematics, is the only form of rationality suited to discuss human problems and human history. As it is, "We are all lost since childhood." Sartre goes so far as to write, "Because nobody has been willing to establish this rationality within experience, I state as a fact—absolutely no one, either in the East or in the West, writes or speaks a sentence or a word about us and our contemporaries that is not a gross error." [7] But if all of us suffer from being imprisoned in language fitted only to discuss objects and scientific entities, the alienation of the black by language is more obvious and more gross. A black poet, unless he is still working within the limits of an isolated tribe, must write in the tongue of his oppressors. This language is pregnant with the echoes of an alien cultural history in which he, as a black, has no part. It is tainted with

[7] *Search for a Method*, p. 111.

racist overtones. Even the great cosmic symbols estrange
and degrade him. "Night" and "black" are symbols of
ignorance and evil. We speak of "a black day," "black
death," a "black heart," the "black mark" against one.

Illustrating his thesis with an abundance of quotations from the poets of the anthology, Sartre argues
that the black writer has attempted to recover his language, to make it his own by two procedures. First, the
poets have developed their own "cosmic sexuality." Sartre quotes three lines from Senghor,

Oho! Congo, reclining on your bed of forests, Queen over
   broken Africa
Let the phalluses of the mountains raise high your flag,
For you are a woman, by my head, by my tongue, for you
   are a woman by my belly.[8]

And these words from Rabéarivelo,

the blood of the earth, the sweat of the rock
and the sperm of the wind.[8]

Expressing through this neoprimitive symbolism a sense
of a natural alignment between the instinctual vitality
of man and of nature, the poet uses language to re-
capture the world for himself.

A second method is to use language surrealistically,
to wrench words away from their ordinary connotations
so as to "strip them of their white underclothes" and
restore them to themselves. (I think, by the way, we
may find a different but related manifestation of this
attempt to recover language in what is happening to
language in America. Both in the writing of black writ-

[8] *Anthologie de la nouvelle poésie nègre et malgache de
langue française, précédée de Orphée noir par Jean-Paul Sartre*,
edited by Léopold Sédar Senghor (Paris: Presses Universitaires
de France, 1969).

ers and in the new counterculture, we find words, expressions, even new grammatical forms of speech which, after decades of being condemned as belonging to uneducated ghetto dwellers, are gradually enriching and transforming accepted language.)

Sartre acknowledges that the black poets are expressing an antiracist racism. He sees it as a necessary stage toward a new society in which each man and woman may dare to be the unique person he or she wants to become.

Negritude appears as the weak stage of a dialectical progression: the thesis is the theoretical and practical assertion of White supremacy; the negating moment is the positing of Negritude as an antithetic value. But this negative moment is not sufficient by itself, and the Blacks who make use of it know this very well. They aim at preparing the synthesis, or human realization, in a society without race. Thus Negritude exists in order to effect its own destruction; it is passage and not destination, means and not final end.[9]

It is not by chance, Sartre says, that "the most ardent celebrants of Negritude are at the same time militant Marxists." Comparing them to Orpheus, who embraces Eurydice only to feel her vanishing from his arms, Sartre quotes from a poem by Jacques Roumain.

Africa, I watch over your memory, Africa
you are in me
like the thorn in the cut
like the guardian fetish in the village center
make of me the stone of your sling,

[9] *Anthologie de la nouvelle poésie nègre et malgache*, p. xli. Sartre's essay has been published separately in English: *Black Orpheus*, translated by S. W. Allen. (No place or date of publication is given, but the paper cover bears the imprint "Présence Africaine.")

of my mouth the lips of your wound
of my knees the broken columns of your humiliation
and yet
I want to be only of your race
workers peasants of every land [10]

Writing *Black Orpheus* in the mid-nineteen-forties, Sartre is acutely aware of the concrete structures which stifle a freedom which tries to "inscribe its being" in the world. Significantly, and understandably in the context, he lays stress on the subjective attitude of blacks who are struggling to change the existing situation. A significant contrast appears if we look at an example from the *Critique* that also illustrates a particular stage in the racial struggle. Instead of a poet, we have a colored member of an air-force ground crew who is forbidden by law to become a pilot. Rebelling against this unjust restriction, he steals a plane. His act can result only in his death. Earlier Sartre might have emphasized the heroism of the choice as a demonstration of human freedom in extreme situations. Now, without playing down the tragic, he emphasizes the ineffectiveness of a personal revolt which leads only to death. Primarily, he has chosen the example to show how even a unique individual action reveals the social and historical context. The mechanic's choice expresses the condition of the class of which he is a member and the precise stage of its self-consciousness. His act illuminates the situation of a class which has acquired a certain technological sophistication but which has not so far found adequate instruments for collective action; as yet it can refuse its condition only by rejecting life itself as "impossible to live." It is meaningless to talk of freedom when a person's only choice is between slaving to earn a mere

[10] *Anthologie de la nouvelle poésie nègre et malgache.*

subsistence or dying, or when an adolescent can see that all but a small remnant of potential careers are cut off from him either by law or by lack of means for his education. Besides these obvious impediments, Sartre stresses the way in which we express our class even in revolting against it and without being aware of the fact. In order to refuse to be a contented bourgeois, one must first *be* a bourgeois; the bourgeois who rebels initiates a bourgeois rebellion.

In an important interview published in 1969 by the English periodical *New Left Review* under the title "Itinerary of a Thought," Sartre commented on the significant changes in his thought since the appearance of *Being and Nothingness.*[11] One of the interviewers remarked on the fact that whereas an entirely different vocabulary was employed in the *Critique,* the recently published excerpts of Sartre's forthcoming study of Flaubert juxtaposed many of these new concepts alongside terms reappearing from *Being and Nothingness.* Sartre was asked about the relation between the two works. Remarking that "the basic question here, of course, is my relationship to Marxism," he clarified his position with respect to freedom, subjectivity, and the unconscious. By his own account Sartre had been shocked to reread some of what he had written a couple of decades earlier. He quoted from a prefatory note to a collection of his plays. " 'Whatever the circumstances, and wherever the site, a man is always free to choose to be a traitor or not.' When I read this, I said to myself: it's incredible, I actually believed that!" Sartre goes on to explain his former overoptimism. Although his experi-

---

[11] This interview was published in abbreviated form under the title "An Interview with Sartre," *The New York Review of Books,* March 26, 1970.

ence as unwilling soldier and then prisoner of war had reminded him of the extent to which man lives among things (Being-in-the-world is one of the dimensions of the For-itself), Sartre was caught up in the "experience of heroism"—"Not my own, of course"—which was offered by the militants in the Resistance. "The problem then was solely that of physical endurance—it was not the ruses of history or the paths of alienation. A man is tortured: what will he do?" This myth of heroism was false, Sartre claims, at least if it is taken to represent the human condition as such. The true experience for Sartre came after the war, and it was the experience "of society." During these years he began to think of man as wholly conditioned by the society in which he lives. While this kind of thinking may be Marxist, it is not determinism. Sartre goes on to say,

The idea which I have never ceased to develop is that in the end one is always responsible for what is made of one. Even if one can do nothing else besides assume this responsibility. For I believe that a man can always make something out of what is made of him. This is the limit I would today accord to freedom: the small movement which makes of a totally conditioned social being someone who does not render back completely what his conditioning has given him. Which makes of Genet a poet when he had been rigorously conditioned to be a thief.

Summing up the process by which Genet accepted and then transformed his position as thief and outcast, Sartre states that such freedom is not a triumph. "For Genet, it simply marked out certain routes which were not initially given." It appears that what is left of freedom (and I myself insist that if it is enough to transform Genet from thief to poet, it is still significant) refers to the irreducible subjectivity in each one of us. Sartre, however, goes on to say that for him today "subjectivity" and "objectivity" are "entirely useless notions." The subjectivity of *Being and Nothingness* has been restricted to "the small margin in an operation whereby an interiorization re-exteriorizes itself in an act." By the time of the *Critique* Sartre prefers to say, "Everything is objective. The individual interiorizes his social determinations: he interiorizes the relations of production, the family of his childhood, the historical past, the contemporary institutions, and he then re-exteriorizes these in acts and options which necessarily refer us back to them. None of this existed in *L'Être et le néant.*"

How does all of this conditioning take place? Is it unconscious? Sartre seems at first to modify his former view of Freud and then makes it clear that a wide gap still separates his own position on psychoanalysis from the traditional Freudian approach. He begins by recognizing that both Marx and Freud emphasize external conditioning. He acknowledges that his own upbringing in a French petty-bourgeois family made it impossible for him to appreciate either Marx or Freud on first encounter. But only the discovery of Marx was a "true discovery." At first, says Sartre with a touch of humor, the Cartesian rationalism which dominated his education would not allow him to take seriously the complex irrational processes described in Freud's *The Psychopathology of Everyday Life.* In any case he was preoccupied with a quite different undertaking, and Sartre's description of it is very important. He explains in the interview that he wanted "to provide a philosophical foundation for realism. Which in my opinion is possible today, and which I have tried to do all my life. In other words, how to give man both his autonomy and his reality among real objects, avoiding idealism without lapsing into a mechanistic materialism."

To give full weight to the autonomous consciousness and to the world within which consciousness exists —this is the goal of Sartre's philosophy early and late. Yet there is no question that his view of how the two interact was modified with the passing of time. Sartre speaks critically of his early theory as a "rationalist philosophy of consciousness." "*Being and Nothingness* is a monument of rationality. But in the end it becomes an irrationalism, because it cannot account rationally for those processes which are 'below' consciousness and which are also rational, but lived as irrational." Sartre's quarrel with the Freudians centers around the problem of whether their theory can account rationally for processes which are still rational even though they are below the level of consciousness. Sartre claims that it cannot. He blames them for confusing mechanistic explanations with finalism. Unconscious activity, for Freud, is purposeful but explained in language which is biological and physiological. Sartre professes himself to be still shocked by this aspect of Freud and unwilling to accept the "mythology of the unconscious" which is its product.

If there are processes "below consciousness," what are we to call them if not subconscious? And how does Sartre avoid falling right back into the Freudian concept of an unconscious? Sartre had always acknowledged "the *facts* of disguise and repression." Earlier he had tried to account for them, as we have seen, by the interplay of reflective and nonreflective consciousness and by bad faith. In the *Critique* he begins to explore the possibilities of a method which will enable us to understand the development of a person—demonstrated psychoanalytically—in conjunction with the structures of society and the movement of history, a method which has finally come into full bloom in Sartre's gigantic study of Flaubert. Speaking of the latter, Sartre says in the interview,

I have replaced my earlier notion of consciousness (although I still use the word a lot), with what I call *le vécu*—lived experience . . . which is neither the precautions of the preconscious, nor the unconscious, nor consciousness, but the terrain in which the individual is perpetually overflowed by himself and his riches, and consciousness plays the trick of determining itself by forgetfulness.

The key to what Sartre means by *le vécu* lies in his comment on a self-revealing sentence by Flaubert: "You are doubtless like myself, you all have the same terrifying and tedious depths." Sartre remarks,

What could be a better formula for the whole world of psychoanalysis, in which one makes terrifying discoveries, yet which always tediously come to the same thing? His awareness of these depths was not an intellectual one. He later wrote that he often had fulgurating intuitions, akin to a dazzling bolt of lightning in which one simultaneously sees nothing and sees everything. Each time they went out, he tried to retrace the paths revealed to him by this blinding light, stumbling and falling in the subsequent darkness.

Sartre goes on to explain that Flaubert's account revealed his relationship "with what is ordinarily called the unconscious and what I would call a total absence of knowledge but a real comprehension." *Le vécu*, lived experience, is "the ensemble of the dialectical process of psychic life, in so far as this process is obscure to itself because it is a constant totalization, thus necessarily a totalization which cannot be conscious of what it is."

Totalization is a key concept in the *Critique* and essential to dialectical reason as such. Although it has absorbed certain connotations derived from Marxist dialectic, "totalization" is basically a synthesis of two ideas presented by Sartre in his description of consciousness. First, every act of consciousness functions as a unification of past and present experience simultaneously with the organization of the external situation within which a consciousness finds itself. To be aware of oneself "in situation" is to assume (we could almost say to become) a total point of view on the world and one's role within it. In addition, we recall that each consciousness is aware that it is an object to others. At every moment the totalization which I am and which I reify, or objectify, in the world by my acts forms part of a larger whole. The unification which I have imposed is in turn totalized by the immediate group of which I am a member, and this group in turn is totalized by other groups and so on ad infinitum till we reach the overall story of mankind and the totalizing attempt of the historian to interpret it.

Le vécu is the lived process by which each person effects his own totalization by perpetually projecting himself out of the past toward his chosen future and always within the compass of a world already worked on by others. In the psychological context, I think we can best understand it if we recall Sartre's early concept of the choice of being. This was a person's basic orientation toward Being, the For-itself's choice of a particular mode of existing in the world. It could be formulated abstractly as a specific form of attempting to realize the unattainable In-itself-for-itself, but it could also be seen concretely as a manifestation of how one apprehended oneself in relation to time, space, the Other, and all the rest of the givens of the human condition.

In the case of Baudelaire, for example, Sartre tried

to show that the poet chose his life as a destiny, attempted to live his life backward, thought of himself as one who had been ejected from Paradise as a child and marked with an irreparable flaw, a defect which simultaneously served as a distinguishing mark of difference on which he prided himself and yet which constituted his existence as a Fall. All of this was a reaction to the specific fact of his mother's remarriage, but Sartre attempts to show that it is the result of the complex activity of a free consciousness in the world; it is not reducible to an Oedipus complex which is taken as an original given and interpreted in terms still tinged with biological determinism. If Baudelaire may be accurately said to have had an Oedipus complex, this is a fact to be explained and not an explanation.

But while the biographer or psychoanalyst may hope to uncover the choice of being conceptually, impersonally, and on the basis of empirical evidence, we must remember that this is not how the choice was made by the person who lived it. He *is* his choice of being, for his choice of being *is* the way that his consciousness relates itself to the world and organizes its experiences. Sartre recognized this point in *Being and Nothingness* and emphasized that one could not simultaneously live the choice and view it objectively from the outside. To do so would be like trying to focus a telescope on its own mechanism. Or it would be to grasp reflectively the nonreflective consciousness while *being* that consciousness. Nevertheless, Sartre's insistence that we are all aware that the choice might have been different and that in fact a person may make a new choice (as in the "rebirth" of a religious conversion) always suggested (more, I am sure, than Sartre intended) that the choice could be slipped in or out of like a garment. Perhaps the difficulty stems from the fact that the instant which evokes the rupture between past and present was represented as making too clean a cut, as if time stopped for a moment. In speaking of *le vécu*, Sartre stresses that the totalization never stops. At every moment a consciousness is in process of adding new experience to old and thus totalizing itself. "One can be conscious of an external totalization, but one cannot be conscious of a totalization which also totalizes consciousness."

Sartre's claim that *le vécu* is susceptible of comprehension but never of knowledge seems to me to account, in terms of concrete psychological experience, for the fact that all consciousness is self-consciousness. Consciousness is aware (of) itself as it totalizes, but this self-awareness is not knowledge. Sartre consistently reserves "knowledge" for an objective realization of the world and one's relation to it. Knowing is a solid bridge between the For-itself and the In-itself. Sartre says that the truth of such moments of comprehension as Flaubert described may be partially retained in such symbols as one uses in dreams. One cannot return to them for objective knowledge any more than one can learn about an external object by scrutinizing the mental image one has of it. This position becomes clearer when Sartre goes on to speak of the neurosis. He explains that he has attempted to "surpass the traditional psychoanalytic ambiguity of psychic facts which are both teleological and mechanical by showing that every psychic fact involves an intentionality which aims at something, while among them a certain number can only exist if they are comprehended, but neither named nor known." In response to a decisive event in childhood, a psychic "wound," a person develops a complex system of reactions to take care of the situation. But since they are essentially a disguise rather than an overcoming or curing, their purposeful activity is effective only so long as it is not subjected to analysis and open confrontation. We have here still the bad faith which Sartre spoke of so many years before, the lie to oneself. But the new theory of *le vécu* shows more effectively the way in which the liar is genuinely the dupe of his own lies.

Sartre's later theory is certainly a modification of his earlier view of freedom. Even when we do make a new choice of being, there are dragged along, so to speak, many of the opaque, unexamined ingredients which were there before. The furniture of the room has mostly been rearranged, even though new things are there and some of the old have been pushed out. Speaking informally and nontechnically, Sartre says at the end of *The Words* that he himself has changed; he goes so far as to declare that the child he once was had been dissolved in quicklime, thanks to the habit he developed of "thinking against himself." We might ask whether a choice of being which requires thinking against oneself does not also involve a particular focusing of the telescope and an afterimage of what went before even as one moves the instrument. Sartre would easily acknowledge this. "One gets rid of a neurosis, one isn't cured of oneself. . . . The traits of the child are still in the quinquagenarian." Yet we may note that for Sartre the freedom of consciousness has always resided in the possibility of taking a new point of view on the objects one "intends" —both in the external and in the internal landscape. This belief of his, at least, has not changed.

In the *Critique* Sartre argues that if we really want to understand a person, we must seek to know him "totally as an individual and yet totally as an expression of his time." If we seek to grasp the personality of

Flaubert, we must know how Flaubert differs from his neighbors; this means that we must find out also what he shares with his neighbors. So far we have been concerned primarily with Sartre's attempt to reinsert the individual project into the heart of Marxism, but we would misrepresent the *Critique* if we created the impression that it is primarily about the individual, even though in the framework of a Marxist interpretation.

The aim of dialectical reason is not only to understand the development and meaning of a particular life but to apprehend the movement of history. The method which Sartre seeks to establish will integrate sociology and psychoanalysis in its study of an individual. But this "regressive-progressive" method, as Sartre calls it, is designed primarily for the sake of understanding the social structure. He acknowledges here the influence of a Marxist, Henri Lefebvre, who, in Sartre's opinion, "has provided a simple and faultless method for integrating sociology and history in the perspective of a materialist dialectic" (*Search for a Method*, p. 51). To put it another way, the regressive-progressive method studies social phenomena both horizontally, bringing to light their interrelations at a given period, and vertically, showing how they manifest the effects of evolving historical events.

Sartrean dialectic is not totally removed from the dialectic of either Hegel or Marx. Sartre continues to see new movements in history as the consequences of existing contradictions which demand to be transcended in a new synthesis. He himself has acknowledged his debt to Hegel by pointing out that both he and Hegel see Truth as something which becomes or emerges in the flow of events and that this evolving Truth is always a Totalization in process (p. xxxiv). But Sartre's philosophy lacks the idealist premise which supports Hegel's dialectical world process. Similarly, Sartre rejects the implied "laws of history" and the metaphysical implications of Marxist dialectical materialism whereby forces outside living men and women direct and determine the course of History. Essentially, dialectical Reason for Sartre is simply the continuing process of totalization. But we must remember that for him this Reason is something more than the mere order of our thoughts. Both the individual life and the movement of society proceed dialectically. Dialectical Reason is a relation between Being and Knowing. It is the only appropriate approach by which human beings, who are—individually and collectively—a perpetual process of self-making by means of totalization, can hope to understand themselves and their history and to plan for their future. Dialectical Reason, because it is based on the recognition of contradictions and transcending syntheses, is the only rational process which can attempt to do justice to man, a being whose very nature is paradoxical.

The main body of the *Critique* analyzes the development of the group which is capable of concerted historical action. Although it would be difficult to conceive of these more than seven hundred pages of abstract theory as intrinsically dramatic, the basic theme of the book almost suggests the rise and fall of classic tragedy. Sartre analyzes the structures which make it difficult for the group-in-fusion to emerge on the stage of history, its brief moment of triumph, and the forces which bring about its gradual disintegration and failure. Indeed, if we were to restrict ourselves to the contents of the *Critique* alone, we might be tempted to conclude that failure for the group is as inevitable as the frustration of attempts at satisfying individual human relations seemed to be in *Being and Nothingness*. But just as the latter were analyzed in the context of bad faith and a mistaken pursuit of the missing God, so we must note that the *Critique* presupposes a milieu of scarcity which it is the aim of Marxism to overcome. Obviously we cannot, in a brief discussion, do justice to Sartre's tightly reasoned argument, nor can we consider all its important implications. What may be most profitable in our present enterprise is to look at the skeletal outline of the nature and history of the communal group and to see how the new structures described derive from, or contrast with, the analysis of human relationships which Sartre presented many years earlier.

In the *Critique* Sartre scarcely mentions Being-in-itself and Being-for-itself, but their presence is everywhere felt. Just as we never meet pure matter except abstractly, so Being, without consciousness, and consciousness, without a specific historical setting, are fit objects for philosophical analysis but not for sociopolitical theory. The two regions of Being are replaced by praxis and the pratico-inerte. Praxis is still very close to the project, which was all but synonymous with a Being-for-itself, but it is not quite the same. Praxis is any purposeful activity, whether of individual or group; it is always action in the world. The pratico-inerte is the world of worked-over matter in which praxis inscribes itself. It includes the physical universe, and Sartre has much more to say now about the way in which material things by their presence or absence circumscribe my action or "steal it from me." This change is illustrated by the shift from stress on the "coefficient of resistance" in things to the "counterfinalities" which acts may evoke. "Coefficient of resistance" suggests simply that which must be overcome by a freedom in process of realizing itself. A "counterfinality" is a result opposite to that which I expected; it may refer to my missing a target when the wind makes the arrow deviate from its course, or (Sartre's example) to what happens when a group of peasants strip a hillside of trees in order to create more cultivable acres and effect only further erosion of their land. The pratico-inerte includes far more than the physical world. It is the whole weight of the social environment, the prevailing customs and institutions, the public media, the very language I speak.

Two other shifts in emphasis are important. Sartre had often referred to the For-itself as being desire as well as choice. Desire suggests an openness, a reaching out for a chosen fulfillment. In the later work desire is ignored, and the stress is on need, which is not freely chosen. With these things in mind, Sartre can say that the truth of a man is his wages, his work, for the external world in which he lives is like a map in which certain roads are open and others are marked "No entrance" or, perhaps worse, "No exit." All these patterns are determined by one thing—scarcity. The historical process is unintelligible, says Sartre, unless we understand that it contains within it a permanent element of negativity which is both external and internal to man —the perpetual possibility of my being the one who causes others to die or is made to die by them. Within the milieu of scarcity, some are expendable. Society chooses its undernourished and its dead. It is obvious, he claims, that under these conditions every society is based on violence, not merely the violence resulting from the wars and oppressions of historical conflict, but an ingrained violence which permeates the entire social system but which was not planned and is seldom recognized. Here, of course, Sartre makes the point which has become a central issue in the proclamations of militant revolutionary groups—that their own resort to violence is justified by the violence existing in the established system. It is not economic laws which are pitiless, but men. "It is freedom which limits freedom" (p. 361). But what makes of freedom a damnation is the fact that man's creative work, his life, is poured out in efforts which do not reflect his being back to him, which make him "the product of his product," which alienate him from himself.

In the milieu of scarcity, across the pratico-inerte, the prevailing social relation is seriality. Sartre introduces the idea of the series with the example of a queue of people waiting for a bus. Although each one has—or we could even say *is*—an individual project, there is nothing which truly unites all these projects. Instead, there is a "plurality of solitudes." A passive unity exists in the pratico-inerte: the bus itself, its prescribed route, the convention which requires that people stand in a line and abide by the principle of "first come, first served." There is even an implied threat against those who might refuse. But the relation among the prospective passengers is basically numerical. They are personally interchangeable within this temporary unity. Only their position in the line in relation to the number of seats, which *may not be enough*, distinguishes one from the other. This analogy would hold, says Sartre, for almost all social relations in today's world, whether we think of the members of a nation, the residents of a city, the student body of a university. It is true of any collection of people so long as they are not so caught up in common praxis that we may say of each one that his own project and that of every other member of the group is precisely the group project.

Seriality is lived amid collectives. The collective is a particular structure within the pratico-inerte, a passive structure of worked-over matter. We could possibly call the transportation system a collective, but Sartre is more concerned with collectives which exhibit this same sort of passive unity in the realm of thought and attitudes, of lived experience. When millions of people watch the same television program, we are in the presence of a collective; the viewers constitute a series. They are not present to one another but to the same object. A newspaper is a collective, as is the nation. So is the intangible "public opinion" which both puts a book on the best-seller list and, by influence, keeps it there. Social class is also a collective as long as its members remain a series. What we call "consciousness raising" is precisely the attempt to overcome serialization, to transform passive, external unity into the common action of a group. The series is characterized by impotence, isolation, and alienation. Each one is other to all the others. If the series is to give way to the group-in-fusion, several things are necessary. There must be some modification in the external situation which both causes the attitudes of the members to change and leads them to overcome the separation which, physically or psychologically, had isolated them from one another. Most often it is a specific crisis which proposes a definite goal—such as the taking of the Bastille, which Sartre chooses as an illustration.

The concept of the group-in-fusion poses the question of group consciousness and of the "We." Sartre had not ignored these in *Being and Nothingness*, but his discussion of the *Nous* (including both the "We-subject" and the "Us-object") was brief and superficial. Furthermore, he quite clearly then regarded group relations as peripheral and secondary compared with the subject-object relationships he had analyzed so extensively. After examining these others briefly, he reasserted that "the essence of the relation between consciousnesses is not the *Mitsein* (being-with) but conflict." (The reference to *Mitsein* is, of course, a thrust at Heidegger.) Certainly in the *Critique*, Sartre has gone far beyond this position in his concept of the group-in-fusion. Nevertheless, I think we may see the germs of the later theory in certain almost offhand observations in the earlier work, and I do not believe that there is any contradiction between the notion of the group-in-fusion and Sartre's original view of the nature of individual consciousness.

In *Being and Nothingness* Sartre began his discussion of group awareness with the "Us-object," giving an example which I assume he derived from O'Neill's play *The Hairy Ape*. The Us-object is experienced "in shame as a community alienation. This is illustrated by that significant scene in which convicts choke with anger and shame when a beautiful woman comes to visit their ship, and sees their rags, their labor, and their misery. We have here a common shame and a common alienation." [p. 415] The experience is transient and cannot by itself result in action. As long as the objects of the Look of the Third remain objects, they are paralyzed by finding in themselves only what the Third sees. (Sartre has put this insight to effective dramatic use in *The Respectful Prostitute*. The prostitute and the Negro, though they can see themselves as the victims of injustice, have so internalized the judgment of the white bourgeois that they are inhibited by their own self-image.) Sartre relates the awareness of the Us-object specifically to class consciousness. In almost Marxist terms, he points out that workmen, united in making things for the use of others—not for themselves—find their unity as an Us-object. So long as they continue to complain about economic conditions which they assume to be inevitable, they are objects before the exploiters. Later Sartre would say that their relation is one of seriality. In *Being and Nothingness* he remarks acutely that the feeling of the individual workmen, either as isolated members of a class or in the experience of the Us-object, cannot be adequately translated as "working for you"—the boss or the capitalist or the rich. It is rather "working for them." The Third is "they." (In the *Critique*, the lack of even direct negative reciprocity is characteristic of the alienating pratico-inerte.)

In *Being and Nothingness* Sartre realized that the recognition of being a part of an Us-object carried in it the possibility of transforming itself, under favorable conditions, into a We-subject, and he noted that in the class struggle, the individual member of the Us-object no longer seeks to recover himself as a subject "I" but rather to transform the oppressors into "They as objects" or "Them." At this point one feels that Sartre might logically have continued with the kind of argument he offered later in *Black Orpheus*. Unfortunately, he moved instead into a rather unprofitable discussion of how some persons have made the futile attempt to see all humanity as an Us-object before God. Approaching the question of the structure of the We-subject, he started from a new angle, keeping it within the context of the ephemeral and insignificant experiences which come when "we" witness an amusing incident on the street before our café or watch a theatrical performance or follow the directions for using the instruments which have been manufactured for "us." Only his example of the rowing team seems to offer something a bit more significant, and even here Sartre speaks of it as simply the momentary merging of projects which touch briefly and tangentially. In any case the "we" is psychological, not ontological like the conflict of the subject and object sides of our consciousnesses. So far as class consciousness is concerned, Sartre points out only that there is no "we" of the oppressors inasmuch as their strategy has always been to deny the reality of the class structure, to stress rather that all must work together for the national interest and other such mystifications.

But there is one highly significant paragraph in which I think Sartre has made suggestions that point beyond what he himself was capable of thinking at the time he wrote it. While still insisting that the psychological experience of the We-subject is not based on any true *Mitsein* and that its value is only that of a symbol of metaphysical unity, he says that as an ideal "it overcomes the original conflict of transcendences by making them converge in the direction of the world. In this sense the ideal We-subject would be the 'we' of a humanity which would make itself master of the earth." [p. 425] What Sartre says here we find later in the *Critique,* where it is presented as the much more realizable ideal of the group-in-fusion. And we shall see that the union which is realized is accomplished not by a union of consciousnesses but by means of common action in the world outside. In the *Critique,* Sartre might have said what he did say in *Being and Nothingness,* though with far different connotations: "I apprehend through the world that I form part of 'we.' "

As Sartre approaches his analysis of the group-in-fusion, he asserts that a radical difference separates him from sociological anthropologists (such as Durkheim and his followers) who try to see in group consciousness something resembling a metaphysical entity. The group is not a hyperorganism. We must reject any form of organicism. No all-inclusive consciousness exists over and above the individual consciousnesses of the group's members. Sartre says that sociologists have erred in taking the group as a binary relation (individual-community). The bond which unites is ternary.

This perhaps marks the greatest change in Sartre's philosophical vocabulary. Earlier the Third was always an agent of disintegration. Now Sartre says that the group-in-fusion is an ensemble of "Third persons." "I apprehend the group as *my* common reality and simultaneously as a mediation between me and every other third" (p. 404). Thus we no longer find the otherness which characterized the series but reciprocity. Instead of the passive unity of the series, the group-in-fusion is held together by a common praxis. Union is based on free, shared action, not the mutual alienation of the pratico-inerte. In such praxis I am a Third without special status, but I am not an object. There is no Other but only a group in which each Third is myself.

In showing how each of us is a Third in a union of Thirds, Sartre is most successful when he describes the group at the height of its activity. Put in the simplest terms possible, we note that I am able, in the group, to accomplish a project which is my project but which I could not accomplish alone—to take the Bastille, to resist the police, to prevent the enforcement of what I believe to be an unjust law. At this point action is nonreflective. I *am* my project, but this project which I am is exactly that project which every Other is. The group is not my object, and I am not an object to the group. "The group is the communitarian structure of my act" (p. 403). Since at this moment I am wholly in my act, and my act is but a part of a common enterprise, Sartre can say that "the group runs on its hundred legs." It does not matter which of its members performs which particular action. There is, at this stage, not even any one leader. People may shout out orders, exhort all together, or call directions to various persons. "I carry out the 'command,' I am the 'word of order'" (p. 408). We are all united by what we do, out there in the world. My freedom is objectifying itself, but this time the image which is returned to me is still myself; it is not alienated. Using the old Marxist terms, Sartre claims that through the group, man may be released at last from being the product of his product; as the result of action in common, he finds himself now transformed into the "product of the group; that is, inasmuch as the group is freedom—*into his own product*" (p. 639). Thus it is through the group that the individual (the For-itself) is finally freed from otherness, from alienation.

Sartre's description of the group in the white heat of action is to me, at least, convincing and consistent with what he has always said of human consciousness. Although it may wrench the language to speak of the group as being made up of Thirds, each one of whom is "a myself," I think Sartre is right in holding that at such moments the usual sense of "I" and "you" is absent and that the feeling of "myness" has been extended to the point of being qualitatively different from what it normally is. We can all recall instances where in the midst of the group activity, one is suddenly aware of a close friend and pauses to inquire as to his personal reactions apropos of what is going on. But this is to add a second experience to the group experience; it may also be true that at such moments the mutual feeling of both being members of the group-in-fusion puts even the individual encounter beyond the subject-object conflict.

The difficulties of Sartre's concept become most apparent when we attempt to envision the group-in-fusion outside the heat of conflict, as a permanent structure in a society at peace with itself. Here Sartre adds another and important ingredient. Not only does the group achieve the common goal of its members who could not attain it alone, but the group enables each one to fulfill his distinctive individual capacities in a way which he could not do in solitude. Sartre uses the example of a football team, which I find a little unfortunate inasmuch as it still seems to suggest that unity must stem from opposition to a common foe. Even if we change the analogy to something like a symphonic group, we do not get rid of the feeling that we have still not progressed very much beyond the transient experience of the rowing crew, which Sartre had dismissed as insignificant in his earlier discussion of the We-subject. Sartre might perhaps reply that in the milieu of scarcity there is always an enemy. This is all too true if we look at history retrospectively, but it offers little hope. We may find a more positive possibility if we look again at the sentence in which Sartre claims that the group frees man from otherness. "The group is both the most effective *means* to control the material environment within the compass of scarcity, and it is the *absolute end* as pure freedom liberating men from otherness" (p. 639). Scarcity has been the condition within which men have made their history; it ought properly to be the eternal enemy against which men would direct their common praxis. We may recall Sartre's half-ironic statement in

Being and Nothingness, "The ideal We-subject would be the 'we' of a humanity which would make itself master of the earth." In essence, this is both the ideal of the group-in-fusion and the aim of Sartre's Neo-Marxism. Dialectical Reason is not only a method of interpreting history as the perpetual process of overcoming contradictions in a new synthesis, but it is also history becoming aware of itself and making itself as *a* history of humanity rather than as a collective of many histories.

This common enterprise of subduing the material universe is not to be confused with the old picture of man as the ruthless and shortsighted destroyer of nature. Sartre argues that in all interaction with matter, a "transubstantiation" takes place. A human being must, to some degree, make himself a material instrument, a thing, in order to work with things. But in the process the thing takes on a human dimension. One has only to think of the difference between a barren seacoast and a fishing village—or better yet, of the function of gold in the world economy or uranium deposits. The united praxis of overcoming and preventing the return of scarcity might well be likened to Marcuse's ideal of "humanizing nature" rather than to the untrammeled exploitation of natural resources which has been the story up till now.

Sartre's choice of the term "common individual" to describe a member of a society which is truly a group is perhaps regrettable, but the implied ideal of uniting individual fulfillment and community certainly suggests a triumph over serialization. Sartre himself recognized that the real difficulty with the group-in-fusion lies not in a defect in the ideal as such but in sustaining a structure which up until now has proved to be all too fleeting and evanescent. The second half of the *Critique* is concerned with what seems to be the inevitable disintegration of the group and the return of serialization amid collectives. The inherent weakness of the group, Sartre says, is simply the fact that it is not, after all, an organism. At the moment of combat, the group was held together by the presence of the common danger. Each one put into parentheses, so to speak, all those differentiations which did not currently come into play. (Again one is reminded of the rowing team, where only the immediate activity unites the projects of diverse individuals.) Once the danger is past, the formerly passive differences threaten to become divisive. The recollection of the shared experience and recognition that danger may return are sufficient to make the group wish to remain a group. But now suddenly the greatest danger is the threat to the existence of the group itself. The threat has substance, for the external situation and the action in common that it provoked are no longer present. It is necessary to recall them deliberately in order to make them real and effective. (Parenthetically, we may note that this is one origin of the memorial ceremonies in celebration of past events which first solidified the group.) Now the group initiates the vow (*le serment*) and terror. Each one swears to inflict punishment by the group on any member who might seek to destroy its unity. Fraternal terror directed against its own becomes the group's substitute for earlier action against the external enemy. Each one, by vowing to invoke the group's action against anyone, including himself, has now constituted himself as potential object for the group. Not only himself. Everyone who is born into the world today is already presworn. As one is born into the group, one must assume his objectivity before it. Once again violence is built into the structure of things. "Each person's freedom invokes the violence of all against itself and against the freedom of any other Third—as its defense against itself (i.e., against its free potentiality for secession and alienation)" (p. 448).

Sartre discusses at length the manifold ways in which serialization gradually replaces community. The details need not concern us. Speaking generally, we may observe that he does not emphasize those things which stem from human error and weakness but rather the factors which inevitably accompany the existence of human beings in the pratico-inerte. Division of labor, for example, even though it may initially be based on the recognition of differentiation in talent and ability, results in separation of the members from one another, both in space and in the quality of their daily activity. Geographical distance means that certain of the group's representatives will be directly involved in decisions which others, even if approving, will receive passively, after the event. A hierarchy of responsibility develops, and then we see the emergence of a sovereign or chief —either in the form of a single leader or of an executive committee. The time comes when the majority of the members may not trust their leaders, but fear of the consequences of the group's disintegration prevents their voicing their disapproval in effective terms. They obey those in authority because they fear that their neighbors may not obey. Time itself is a disruptive factor. An idea is not the same for the generation which proposes it as for those which receive it. The children of the original founders find themselves living not in a group but in an institution. The series and the collective have returned.

Sartre points up the basic irony in what has happened. The group was brought into existence by real action-in-common in the material world, but it is the necessity of continuing its praxis in the pratico-inerte which ultimately destroys it. "The group, a *praxis* which sinks itself in matter, finds in its materiality—that is, in its becoming-a-process—its true effectiveness. But to the degree that *praxis* is process, the ends proposed lose their teleological character; without ceasing to be ends, strictly speaking, they become destinies." [p. 631] At the final stage we have the bureaucracy of a pyramidal structure. The lower levels are always the objects of the praxis of those above. The power of all authorities rests on the impotence, the separation, the otherness or alienation of the members who make up the series.

Sartre demonstrates how the history of the Soviet Union is the story of the development and disintegration of the group-in-fusion. He explains it in the light of the historical events which all can observe. At the same time he associates the failure of applied political Marxism with the failure of traditional Marxist theory. His hope for the future rests on the possibility of a dialectical approach to history which may unite the correct understanding of social process with appropriate praxis so as to overcome the conflicts arising from scarcity and to allow the emergence of a permanent group in which each "common individual" is also a free self-creating person. Granted that most of the *Critique* has been an analysis of the negative forces which have prevented the realization of this social ideal, the negative moment is essential to a dialectical progression. At least on the theoretical side, the *Critique* is consistent in working toward a synthesis of Marxism and existentialism which Sartre hopes will set Marxism moving again toward the point where it is no longer needed and where human beings need no longer feel that they must be inhuman toward one another.

8

CONCLUSION: SARTRE
AND THE REVOLUTION

回 回 回

There are two critical moments in Sartre's life which he himself has described in terms which suggest that they represent in his eyes a "radical conversion"—though we must certainly not equate either one with the philosophical "conversion" hinted at in *Being and Nothingness* or with the dramatic cleavage some critics have tried to establish between the author of that book and the Sartre who wrote the *Critique*. The first occasion is associated with Sartre's decision late in 1953 to write his autobiography. The 1954 version, he tells us, was a radical denunciation of his early life, quite different from the more sympathetic irony of the published volume ten years later. The crisis was wholly personal and internal. We should look in vain for any one precipitating event either in world history or in Sartre's private life. Sartre himself implies that it was the result of the sudden merging of the two. "At that moment, as the consequence of the turn of political events, I was intensely involved in my relations with the Communist Party. Thrown into the pressure of action, I had a sudden clear insight into the kind of neurosis which had dominated all of my former work." [1] He identified this "neurosis" with his original choice of himself as a

[1] "Jean-Paul Sartre s'explique sur *Les Mots*," *Le Monde*, April 18, 1964.

writer. "The peculiar quality of every neurosis is that it takes itself as natural. I was peacefully assuming that I had been made for writing. Out of the need to justify my existence, I had made an absolute out of literature. It took me thirty years to get myself out of that frame of mind." "I had dreamed my life for almost fifty years," declared Sartre, who was now approaching fifty-nine. "The youngster who dreams of being a boxing champion or an admiral or an astronaut is choosing the real. If a writer chooses the imaginary, it is because he confuses the two domains."

This self-insight brought Sartre to two conclusions: Neither the writer nor literature is privileged. One's life is not justified by writing; nor is one saved by politics, or by anything else. "There is no salvation anywhere." For Sartre, the critical realization was that life offers *no absolute*. It was as though suddenly he found that he was serving the missing God after all, living with the comfortable assurance that so long as he wrote in good conscience, he was serving the cause of human freedom and thereby justifying himself. Now suddenly even the concept of engaged literature is put into question. The engaged writer seeks to justify the particular commitment he makes, but so long as he takes it for granted that writing itself is his proper mission, he is assuming that the writer has a privileged status. I think we can understand how for Sartre himself this change in point of view was both radical and critical. He saw himself and his career both put into question. For the man who has chosen himself as writer, it appears that the only thing necessary is to ensure that one's writing is influential in a chosen direction. Now Sartre asks whether influence is enough. Is it not at times an evasion of more direct action? This question was to come

to full fruition a few years later in more radical statements (and action) by Sartre apropos of the role of the
intellectual at a time of revolution.

For us who observe from the outside, Sartre's shift
in attitude in the mid-fifties seems much less of a water-
shed than it appeared to him. Outwardly the effect on
his career was far less striking than the decision he arrived at in the year 1940 when for the first time he
recognized the obligation to involve himself politically.
In the light of Sartre's prominent role in international
politics in recent years, it comes as something of a shock
to realize that he was almost thirty-five years old before
he so much as took any genuine interest in national elections. His iconoclasm in the thirties was a strictly individual affair. His Marxist sympathies were purely theoretical and mostly submerged in apathy. He was already
hard at work on the theory of consciousness and the
imagination which were to become the backbone of his
philosophy, but his approach to them was highly
academic.

Since 1940 there has been no respite in his political
involvement. After his release from prison, Sartre continued his work on *Being and Nothingness* and developed the interest in the theater which he discovered
with *Bariona*, but he was also working actively in the
Resistance movement during those years. After the war
ended in 1945, he helped launch the monthly periodical
Les Temps modernes, of which he is still editor and in
which he has published a steady succession of articles
on specific political issues. Nor was the engagement a
wholly literary one. Sartre engaged himself tirelessly in
drawing up manifestos, joining in demonstrations, speaking at public meetings, attending political congresses in
other countries as well as inside France, participating

in every way possible, short of actually seeking public office, in domestic and international affairs.

In 1948 he was one of the leaders in trying to form an effective coalition of Leftist parties, the Rassemblement Démocratique Révolutionnaire. The attempt failed, partly because of the more conservative leanings of some of Sartre's associates and partly because the Communists, after initially endorsing the project, refused to cooperate. Despite these frustrations, Sartre was working closely with the Communists in the months preceding the "crisis" of the winter of 1953–54. Two and a half years later he broke with them completely at the time of the Soviet intervention in Hungary. His political activity continued at the same pace. This was the period when he was particularly caught up in protesting the policy of the French Government in Algeria. And, of course, he was finishing the development of his Neo-Marxism in the *Critique*. The change in Sartre's view of the importance of literature did not prevent his continuing to write for the theater. *Nekrassov*, a political satire, was produced in 1955; *The Condemned of Altona*, in 1959; and 1965 saw the production of his adaptation of Euripides' *Trojan Women*.

The truth is that in the interview Sartre gave at the time of the publication of his autobiography in 1964, his statement that literature is not privileged was followed by comments on particular writers which sound very much like the theory of "engaged literature" offered by Sartre in the forties. He deplores the "soft pessimism" of Beckett and speaks scornfully of Robbe-Grillet's concern with purely artistic problems. "Do you think I could read Robbe-Grillet in an underdeveloped country?" But he adds that he could read Kafka in Guinea. "In him I find my own malaise." Basically what he demands is still a commitment on the part of the writer to help man understand himself and the world so that he may change it. "What I ask of [the writer] is that he should not ignore reality and the fundamental problems which are before us: world hunger, the atomic menace, man's alienation." Sartre stated that he himself had begun work on a study of Flaubert, and it is interesting that the reason he gave here for his wanting to write the biography was purely personal. "Because he is the opposite of what I am. One needs to tangle with what challenges one." When the reviewer remarked that after all Sartre had not changed so greatly, he replied, "I have changed like everyone else—within a permanence."

Sartre has not written plays or other fiction since *The Trojan Women*, though as recently as 1969 he implied that his interest in the theater was as keen as ever. His refusal of the Nobel Prize in 1964 may possibly have been related to his rejection of the privileged status of literature, but there were other more pressing reasons. He felt that those who awarded the Nobel Prize had not always been free of political motives—as in the case of Pasternak's *Doctor Zhivago*. But he added that he would similarly have rejected the Lenin Prize if it had been offered him, for he felt that an author ought to speak free of the weight of any established authority. And along with all of this, one suspects that Sartre, on the purely emotional level, disliked becoming known as one on whom the bourgeois world had bestowed its public approval.

In 1965 Sartre canceled the arrangements he had made to come to America to lecture at Cornell University. Basically this was a protest against the United States policy in Vietnam, but the explanation Sartre gave for his refusal showed that his gesture meant more than a protest to the State Department apropos of a specific policy. To those who urged that he ought to take advantage of the opportunity to come and argue the question of Vietnam, he replied that there would be no real dialogue.

Discussion is possible only with those who are ready to put in question the whole American imperialist policy—not only in Vietnam but in South America, in Korea, and in all the countries constituting a "third world"; moreover, discussion is possible only with those Americans who will concede that American policy cannot be changed short of a complete turnover of American society. Now very few, even on the American Left, are ready to go that far.[2]

Sartre has not visited America since then, but he has praised the recent antiwar movement as one of the finest examples of revolutionary activity.

In 1967 Sartre joined with Bertrand Russell in heading the International War Crimes Tribunal. His most important contribution was the address he delivered on the final day of the session, "On Genocide." Among the many documents in which he has written critically of the United States, this is probably the most painful for American readers, whatever their political convictions. Sartre himself seems to have had doubts at first as to whether it was just to accuse the United States of killing Vietnamese *as such* in the same way the Nazis demonstrably planned genocide against the Jews. The finished speech shows no signs of this hesitation, though he points out that the Government pronouncements in this country lack the candor of the Nazi proclamations. There is a deliberate deceiving of the American people

[2] "Why I Will Not Go to the United States," *The Nation*, April 19, 1965.

and perhaps self-deception in their leaders. Are those who propose genocide "thoroughly conscious of their intentions? It is impossible to decide. We would have to plumb the depths of their consciences—and the bad faith of Americans works wonders. There are probably people in the State Department who have become so used to fooling themselves that they still think they are working for the good of the Vietnamese people." [3] Whether initiated deliberately or not, the process of genocide was, to Sartre, historical fact. It was manifest, he claimed, in the wish "to make an example out of Vietnam," to disguise the intention of genocide by offering a choice which was no choice—between extermination or a total capitulation which would ultimately have the same effect on the character of Vietnamese society; and it was displayed in the overt racism of American soldiers.

Sartre has associated Vietnam with the student revolt in France and with the new revolutionary movement all over the world. It was the sight of a small country's ability to stand up to a giant and to hold him off that inspired in minorities everywhere the hope of what united action might accomplish.

May 1968, the time of the student demonstrations in France, marks the second of Sartre's "radical conversions." He regards this as an absolute turning point and obviously believes that it—or comparable developments in other countries—must be regarded as a moment of revelation for all intellectuals. In some ways I feel that this second conversion, although significantly

[3] "On Genocide" is contained in *Against the Crime of Silence. Proceedings of the International War Crimes Tribunal*, edited by John Duffett (New York: Simon and Schuster, 1970), pp. 612–26. It was also published, with a description of the circumstances under which it was written, in *Ramparts* (February, 1968).

connected with a contemporary crisis in the world, is almost a reaffirmation and intensification of Sartre's new insight into himself and his responsibilities as a writer which he described apropos of his experiences in 1953. Perhaps it is precisely because the second is more firmly anchored in specific external events that its effect on his life and career has been more pronounced. What May 1968 meant for him he explains in two interviews.

The first was published in September 1970 in the radical journal *L'Idiot International*, of which Simone de Beauvoir took over at least the titular editorship. The report of the interview is entitled "J.-P. Sartre: the Friend of the People" and is preceded by a quotation from a Maoist publication in which a young intellectual says of himself, "Formerly it seemed to me that only the intellectuals were clean and that compared to them, the workers and peasants were dirty. Having become a revolutionary, I lived among the workers, the peasants and the soldiers of the revolutionary army and gradually I became familiar with them and they with me." The theme of Sartre's discussion is the need for the intellectual to stop working *for* the people and to become one *with* them. What he calls the "classical intellectual" is a person who lives and suffers from a basic contradiction. As a "technician of knowledge," he works conceptually with information and ideas which are universal, true—at least in intention—for all mankind. But his services, whether he is a doctor, lawyer, or teacher, are always addressed to individuals in a particular group or class. Thus he "works in the universal to serve the particular." Awareness of this contradiction is the origin of the intellectual's "unhappy consciousness" or "uneasy conscience." Until the time of the student revolt, Sartre claims, the sensitive intellectual suffered from this contradiction but still believed that he could be useful precisely because his aims were directed toward realizing a universal society in which intellectuals could at last address themselves to a liberated population. Thus, Sartre says, the intellectual creates a good conscience out of a bad conscience, but he is still in bad faith. Selectively he may support the antiwar protest or civil rights for minorities, but he never questions himself and his own position as an intellectual. The events of May 1968 changed all that. Now a professor, especially, realized that if he was not with the students, he was against them; so long as he observed the academic rules of the System, he was supporting the System and the privileges it conferred on him.

Sartre professes no real hope that many established professionals will abandon their careers or even seriously risk them. He places his faith in the "apprentice-intellectuals" who, whether they have achieved their degrees or are still in process of earning them, refuse to accept their position in a society in which a man is defined by his function and his salary. Such a person will not wish "to be an intellectual" but will put his services at the disposal of whatever revolutionary or workers' group may make use of them. Only by serving the masses directly will he hope to realize the "concrete universal." If, for example, he has skill as a journalist, he will no longer simply write himself but will work with others to prepare articles in which the workers themselves may express themselves to other workers. Sartre is emphatic in criticizing the Communists for having kept their cells separate, at most sending out an intellectual to provide information and direction for the workers but never truly living and laboring with them at the same level.

In expressing these revolutionary hopes, Sartre displays his old habit of "thinking against himself." Although he had demonstrated his own good faith by lending his name to the editorship of radical periodicals and had publicly handed out literature which the French government had condemned as subversive, he confessed that at bottom he remained "a classical intellectual." The problem centered around his "Flaubert." For over twenty-five years he had entertained the project of writing this biography.

Then comes May '68. This makes fifteen years that I've been working on it, that I've been inside it. What should I do? Abandon it? That makes no sense, and yet as somebody once said, "Lenin's forty volumes represent an oppression of the masses."

Sartre recognized that his study of Flaubert is not directly accessible to the masses but wondered wistfully whether it was a work which was necessarily destined to be lost in oblivion or might possibly prove to be of use, to be one of those books which, for reasons which we cannot foresee today, may be ultimately "recoverable" for the masses.

It would be easy to respond that it is unlikely that the first three of the planned volumes on Flaubert which have now been published and which add up to close to three thousand pages will ever be read by more than the tiniest fraction of any given generation.[4] On the other hand, who is to say that they may not contribute significantly to the cause of human liberation? Sartre's *Baudelaire* was an attempt to apply existentialist psychoanalysis to a dead poet. At most it served to illustrate

---

[4] *L'Idiot de la famille. Gustave Flaubert de 1821 à 1857* (Paris: Gallimard, Vols. 1 and 2, 1971; Vol. 3, 1972).

Sartre's concept of the "choice of being" and may have influenced some readers to see in Baudelaire a little less of the pathetic victim he himself sought to prove he was. *Saint Genet, comédien et martyr* (*Saint Genet: Actor and Martyr*) examined the process whereby one of society's outcasts made himself into something other than what had been assigned to him. Created a bastard, conditioned to be a thief, his revolt transformed him into a poet. Sartre's application of psychology to Genet has greatly influenced at least one of the leading psychoanalysts, R. D. Laing, and, through him, his many followers. I suspect that Genet himself has not been unaffected by Sartre's account of him. The plays which Genet wrote after Sartre's book appeared seem to fit the pattern there described even better than those which preceded the biography.

L'Idiot de la famille aims higher. Sartre's goal is to combine the psychoanalytical approach with the methods of sociology and historical research in such a way that we may understand both an individual and his society; still more important, we may thus learn to comprehend their interaction. If the method is valid, we may hope not only to find illuminated the life and personality of one great writer but to grasp the very movement of history as the record of projects of many men and women reacting on one another so as to create the common story of mankind. Viewed in this way, Sartre's laborious analysis of Flaubert is both an attempt to interpret history and an effort to make history into the united praxis of humanity. The only true understanding of history is based on dialectical Reason. Each person's life is a perpetual process of totalization. At each moment I totalize—I impose unity and organization on—my present situation in the environment along with my past and future. Every choice, every act is a totalization of my experience in the light of the future which I project. At the same time my experience may be described as a constant process of being subjected to the totalization of others, both of individuals and of groups in an ever widening series of totalizations. The historian attempts to totalize all these totalizations. But here too, "the experimenter is part of the experimental system," as Sartre pointed out long ago in *Being and Nothingness*. The act of interpreting history is itself an action launched toward what is to come. It is simultaneously, Sartre says, a totalizing conservation of the past and an orientation toward the future.

If Sartre has succeeded in demonstrating that the Neo-Marxist interpretation of man in society is the correct one and the only one which points the way to the liberation of man, it seems to me that the writing of his "Flaubert" is genuine political action. For Sartre at the moment, it appears to be not enough. The book still exhibits concern with interpreting the universal theoretically rather than acting directly to bring into existence the "concrete universal." The writing of it was an attempt to influence and not direct action.

Sartre's most radical statements apropos of the role of the intellectual were made in an interview with John Gerassi, published in *The New York Times Magazine* on October 17, 1971. Gerassi opened the interview by saying to Sartre, "You have often told me in recent times that the only viable activity for the intellectual today is the political tract." Then he proceeded to ask Sartre whether his volume on Flaubert was not in itself a contradiction and what Sartre would mean by "viable activity." Sartre replied that his book might indeed be "a form of petty-bourgeois escapism" even though it was "a very political work." He went on to state in very strong terms that the intellectual who believes in the revolution must put himself on the line in immediate action even at the cost of his career or, if need be, his life.

Today it is sheer bad faith, hence counterrevolutionary, for the intellectual to dwell on his own problems, instead of realizing that he is an intellectual because of the masses and through them; therefore, that he owes his knowledge to them and must be with them and in them: he must be dedicated to work for their problems, not his own.

Sartre explained the change effected in him by the events of May 1968 as the transition from being a "left-wing intellectual" (*un intellectuel de gauche*), which he was from 1940 until 1968, to a "leftist intellectual" (*un intellectuel gauchiste*).

The difference is one of action. A leftist intellectual is one who realizes that being an intellectual exempts him from nothing. He forsakes his privileges, or tries to, in actions. It is similar, I think, to what in the U.S. you would call white-skin privileges.

Sartre's program for appropriate action is an expansion of what he described in the earlier interview for *L'Idiot International,* except that there is still more stress on active resistance to authority. He goes so far as to say that he supports recourse to counterviolence as a means of opposing the violence present in the existing system. Yet he gives his own goal as "total revolution without terror." Asked whether he approves of the Weatherman tactics in the U.S., he responds, "Except that the Maos here are less violent and they are not trying to lay the foundation of a revolutionary party but to create condi-

tions which will mobilize the masses from which, and
only from which, such a party will surge. But, you see,
here the conditions are not the same. Here we often
win." Gerassi complains that Sartre's break with Castro
because of the imprisonment of a Cuban poet, Heberto
Padilla, for "counterrevolutionary attitudes" proves that
Sartre still clings to the belief that "intellectuals have a
privileged status." What Sartre would say to this charge
I do not know. To me, his action shows rather that he
is still reluctant to sacrifice individuals to historical
principles.

Just how Sartre would define the program of the
revolution which he supports remains a bit vague. Obviously his position remains fundamentally Marxist; it
is definitely non-Communist. Perhaps it is best to say
that he still follows the guidelines he laid down for the
new revolutionary in 1946: one must work toward resocialization while recognizing that the precise form and
even the specific values of what one seeks to establish
will emerge only in the creative process of bringing them
into existence. Meanwhile for him the revolution is a
reality. It has begun, and he hopes for its eventual success without feeling that there is any fixed, impersonal
process to guarantee its outcome. His feeling of the
urgency for commitment in the contemporary crisis is
foreshadowed in a passage in *Being and Nothingness*,
where, though still a "left-wing intellectual," he wrote
that the war which comes is my war so long as I do
not risk my life to prevent it.

There will be many, even among those who are
willing to accept Sartre's overall *Weltanschauung*, who
will refuse to go along with his "applied philosophy" in
the immediate historical situation. And who is to say

whether Sartre himself may not take time out from the arena to crystallize more clearly, perhaps even differently, his aims in this particular advance toward a projected future? Certainly it is not up to us to predict. Retrospectively, however, I believe that Sartre's career has demonstrated two things conclusively. First, both his life and his work have offered visible proof that good faith is possible. Second, he has been able to construct a positive theory of human relations, consistent with his first analysis of what it means to be an individual consciousness in the world. Conflict is the starting point for personal relationships and for society in the milieu of scarcity. Love is a human triumph, not over the original conditions but within them and in spite of them. Community emerges as men and women struggle together against the common enemy instead of against one another. Sartre has progressed from concern with a man's "choice of being" to preoccupation with the question of how we may bring about a new world in which man may freely be. He does not pretend that the overcoming of scarcity will usher in a millennium, only that it will allow human beings to meet, without oppressive handicaps, the problems which stem from the fact that to be human is to be a self-chosen project. In Sartre's philosophy, freedom is both starting point and ultimate goal.

SUGGESTIONS
FOR FURTHER READING

回 回 回

(*English translations are listed when available*)

BOOKS BY SARTRE

Autobiography

The Words. Translated by Bernard Frechtman. New York: George Braziller, 1964.

Biography

Saint Genet: Actor and Martyr. Translated by Bernard Frechtman. New York: George Braziller, 1963.

Drama

The Condemned of Altona. Translated by Sylvia and George Leeson. New York: Alfred A. Knopf, 1961. (This translation was originally published under the title *Loser Wins*. London: Hamish Hamilton, 1960.)
The Devil & The Good Lord and Two Other Plays. Translated by Kitty Black and by Sylvia and George Leeson. New York: Vintage, 1960.

No Exit and Three Other Plays. Translated by Stuart Gilbert and Lionel Abel. New York: Vintage, 1955.

Novels

Nausea. Translated by Lloyd Alexander. New York: New Directions, 1959.
The Roads to Freedom. A trilogy consisting of *The Age of Reason* and *The Reprieve,* translated by Eric Sutton, and *Troubled Sleep,* translated by Gerard Hopkins. New York: Alfred A. Knopf, 1949, 1947, 1951.

Philosophical works

Being and Nothingness. Translated by Hazel E. Barnes. New York: Washington Square Press, 1966.
Search for a Method. Translated by Hazel E. Barnes. New York: Alfred A. Knopf, 1963.

BOOKS ABOUT SARTRE

Biographical sources

Michel Contat and Michel Rybalka. *Les Écrits de Sartre. Chronologie, bibliographie commentée.* Paris: Gallimard, 1970.
Simone de Beauvoir. *Memoirs of a Dutiful Daughter.* Translated by James Kirkup. New York: World Publishing Company, 1959.
———. *The Prime of Life.* Translated by Peter Green. New York: World Publishing Company, 1962.

————. *Force of Circumstance*. Translated by Richard Howard. New York: G. P. Putnam, 1964.

Critical Discussions

Barnes, Hazel E. *An Existentialist Ethics*. New York: Alfred A. Knopf, 1967.
————. *Humanistic Existentialism*. Lincoln, Neb.: University of Nebraska Press, 1962.
Bauer, George Howard. *Sartre and the Artist*. Chicago: University of Chicago Press, 1969.
Fell, Joseph P. III. *Emotion in the Thought of Sartre*. New York: Columbia University Press, 1965.
Greene, Norman N. *Jean-Paul Sartre: The Existentialist Ethic*. Ann Arbor: University of Michigan Press, 1960.
Laing, R. D., and D. G. Cooper. *Reason and Violence: A Decade of Sartre's Philosophy 1950–1960*. New York: Humanities Press, 1964.
McCall, Dorothy. *The Theatre of Jean-Paul Sartre*. New York: Columbia University Press, 1969.
Sheridan, James F., Jr. *Sartre: The Radical Conversion*. Athens, Ohio: Ohio University Press, 1969.
Thody, Philip. *Jean-Paul Sartre: A Literary and Political Study*. London: Hamish Hamilton, 1960.
Warnock, Mary, ed. *Sartre: A Collection of Critical Essays*. Garden City, N.Y.: Doubleday, 1971.

INDEX